CAMPAIGN • 246

BORODINO 1812

Napoleon's great gamble

PHILIP HAYTHORNTHWAITE   ILLUSTRATED BY PETER DENNIS

Series editor Marcus Cowper

OSPREY PUBLISHING
Bloomsbury Publishing Plc

Kemp House, Chawley Park, Cumnor Hill, Oxford OX2 9PH, UK
29 Earlsfort Terrace, Dublin 2, Ireland
1385 Broadway, 5th Floor, New York, NY 10018, USA
Email: info@ospreypublishing.com
www.ospreypublishing.com

OSPREY is a trademark of Osprey Publishing Ltd

First published in Great Britain in 2012

Print ISBN: 978 1 84908 696 7
ePDF: 978 1 84908 697 4
ePub: 978 1 78096 881 0

Editorial by Ilios Publishing Ltd, Oxford, UK (www.iliospublishing.com)
Page layout by The Black Spot
Index by Sandra Shotter
Maps by www.bounford.com
3D bird's-eye view The Black Spot
Battlescene illustrations by Peter Dennis
Typeset in Myriad Pro and Sabon
Originated by PDQ Media, UK
Printed and bound in Great Britain

FSC
www.fsc.org
MIX
Paper from
responsible sources
FSC® C013604

22 23 24 25 26   12 11 10 9 8 7

www.ospreypublishing.com
To find out more about our authors and books visit our website. Here
you will find extracts, author interviews, details of forthcoming events
and the option to sign-up for our newsletter.

AUTHOR'S NOTE

Many different spellings of proper names may be encountered in modern,
and especially earlier works, involving both places and individuals; for
example, Kolotcha, Kolocha, or Kolotza; Semenovskaya or Semenowskoie;
Krasny, Krasni or Krasnoe; Kutuzov, Kutusow or Kutusof; Uvarov or
Ouwarrow, and countless more. Dates are given according to the Gregorian
calendar used in western Europe; Russia still used the Julian calendar which
in 1812 was 12 days behind the Gregorian.

EDITOR'S NOTE

All the images in this publication come from the author's collection.

ARTIST'S NOTE

Readers may care to note that the original paintings from which the
color plates in this book were prepared are available for private sale.
The Publishers retain all reproduction copyright whatsoever. All enquiries
should be addressed to:

Peter Dennis, Fieldhead, The Park, Mansfield, NOTTS, NG18 2AT, UK
Email: magie.h@ntlworld.com

The Publishers regret that they can enter into no correspondence upon
this matter.

THE WOODLAND TRUST

Osprey Publishing are supporting the Woodland Trust, the UK's leading
woodland conservation charity, by funding the dedication of trees.

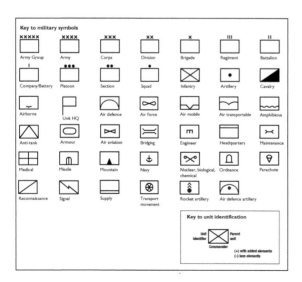

CONTENTS

THE ROAD TO BORODINO   5

CHRONOLOGY   7

OPPOSING COMMANDERS   9
French commanders . The Tsar's generals

OPPOSING PLANS AND FORCES   16
Napoleon's plans . The Tsar's resources . Orders of battle

THE INVASION   27
Smolensk . Kutuzov takes command

THE BATTLE OF BORODINO   40
The battlefield . Napoleon's arrival and the Shevardino Redoubt . The battle begins
The Russian left . The centre . Semenovskaya . The Russian right wing
The fall of the Great Redoubt . The battle ends

THE END OF THE CAMPAIGN   73
The march to Moscow . Moscow . The retreat . The Berezina

AFTERMATH   90

THE BATTLEFIELD TODAY   92

BIBLIOGRAPHY   94

INDEX   95

The strategic situation at the beginning of the campaign

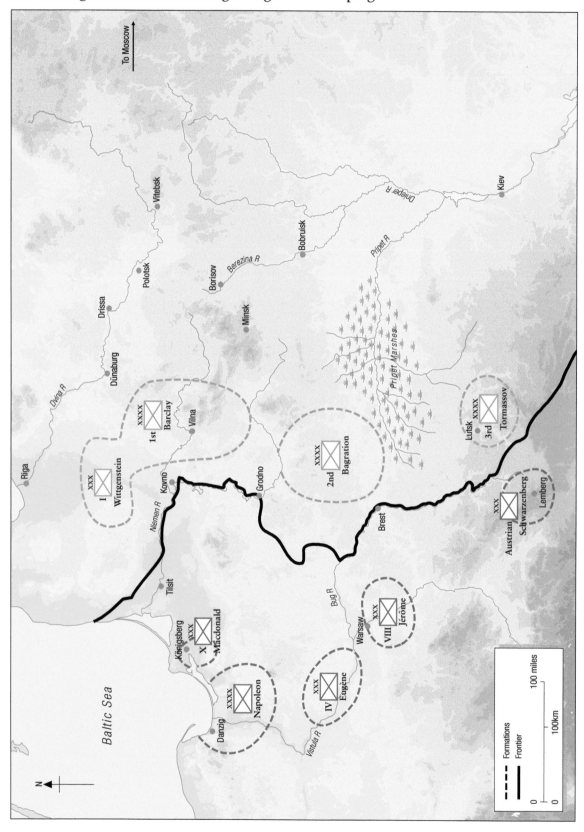

THE ROAD TO BORODINO

In 1812 Napoleon was at the height of his political and military authority; in this portrait he wears his favourite uniform, that of the Chasseurs à Cheval of the Imperial Guard. (Print after Horace Vernet)

In the year 1811 it appeared that Napoleon Bonaparte was at the zenith of his power. He ruled France as emperor, northern Italy as king, and had recently annexed the Kingdom of Holland. His brothers ruled in Spain and northern Germany, his brother-in-law in the Kingdom of Naples, and much of the remainder of Germany was bound into the Rheinbund (or 'Confederation of the Rhine'), an organization of satellite states of which the principal purpose was to support the French emperor. Napoleon's three Continental rivals appeared neutered: Prussia, defeated catastrophically in 1806, was reduced to temporary impotence; Austria, defeated in 1809, was in an alliance with Napoleon cemented by his marriage to the daughter of the Austrian emperor; and Russia, defeated in 1807, was also in an alliance following the Treaty of Tilsit that concluded Franco-Russian hostilities.

Napoleon's situation, however, was not as secure as it might have appeared. His most intractable enemy, Britain, was not only supporting Spanish resistance to the rule of Joseph Bonaparte, but continued to conduct a naval campaign directed against Napoleon's commerce. His attempt to strangle British trade by denying it access to ports under his control, the so-called 'Continental System', had already proved a contributory factor to the beginning of the Peninsular War, and by 1811 was imposing a major strain upon his relations with Russia.

Tsar Alexander I of Russia seemed to his contemporaries to be an intriguing contradiction. Ruler of the most autocratic state in Europe, one which still maintained serfdom, he also possessed liberal ideas and initially seems to have admired Napoleon, an admiration heightened by their meeting at the conference that decided the Treaty of Tilsit. Alexander initially implemented the Continental System, even to the extent of entering a formal state of war against Britain, but it had a destructive effect upon Russian commerce, and it had become obvious that Alexander was conniving at evasions of the system. Other factors also contributed to the worsening of Franco-Russian relations, including the establishment by Napoleon of a client state in Poland, the Duchy of Warsaw, which aroused much suspicion among Russians who regarded Poland as almost their own fiefdom. Napoleon was seen as working against Russian expansionist aspirations in the Balkans and other regions of the Ottoman Empire and Persia, and another cause of friction was Napoleon's annexation of Oldenburg, whose duke was the Tsar's brother-in-law. The appointment of Napoleon's marshal Jean-Baptiste Bernadotte as crown prince and heir-apparent to the throne of Sweden – though he was actually mistrusted by Napoleon – made it appear

Tsar Alexander I (1777–1825), one of the most influential personalities in European politics. (Engraving by H. Mayer)

that he was attempting to surround Russia with enemies, causing even more disquiet among the Tsar and his advisors.

Ostensibly Napoleon claimed to believe that the Tsar was planning to make war on France, despite assurances to the contrary from his ambassadors to Russia, Armand de Caulaincourt and, from 1811, Jacques-Alexandre Lauriston. By the late summer of 1811 Napoleon seems to have been convinced that a new war against Russia was necessary, to confirm the campaign against British commerce and to put a rival in his place. Subsequently Napoleon claimed that 'this famous war, this bold enterprise, was perfectly involuntary in my part. I did not wish to fight; neither did Alexander; but being once in presence, circumstances urged us on, and fate accomplished the rest'; and that 'it was a war of good sense and true interests; a war for the repose and security of all; it was purely pacific and preservative... I had no wish to obtain any new acquisition; and I reserved for myself only the glory of doing good, and the blessings of posterity... I never acted more disinterestedly, and never better merited success.'[1] Such claims ring hollow, especially for the countless thousands who died in consequence of his actions.

For the planned enterprise, Napoleon would demand support from all his allies, including from Austria and, albeit unwillingly, from Prussia; yet in the period before the commencement of hostilities it was Russia that achieved most diplomatically. Far from presenting a pro-French threat, Bernadotte edged cautiously towards an accommodation with Russia, initially adopting a stance of neutrality which ultimately developed into an alliance against Napoleon. Russia's smouldering dispute with the Ottoman Empire over the principalities of Bessarabia, Moldavia and Wallachia was resolved, with British mediation, by the Treaty of Bucharest in May 1812, which permitted the transfer of Russian troops from the Ottoman frontier to the focus of the looming war against France. Finally, in July 1812 Russia concluded an alliance with Britain. By these measures the Tsar was able to focus all his attention upon resisting Napoleon's forthcoming attack.

1. Las Cases, comte de, *Memoirs of the Life, Exile and Conversations of the Emperor Napoleon,* London 1836, Vol. IV, pp. 109, 19–20.

CHRONOLOGY

1807

7–8 February	Napoleon defeats Russian army of Levin Bennigsen at Eylau.
14 June	Napoleon defeats Bennigsen again at Friedland.
7–9 July	Treaty of Tilsit, sealing peace between France and Russia, by which Russia acceded to the Continental System and recognized the Duchy of Warsaw.

1812

24 March	as tension between Russia and France comes to a head, Russia agrees an alliance with Sweden, beginning to gather allies.
15 May	as he prepares for the campaign, Napoleon is received by the King of Saxony near Dresden; other allies and clients attended subsequently.
28 May	Treaty of Bucharest between Russia and the Ottoman Empire, allowing Russia to concentrate her military resources against the looming invasion by Napoleon.
29 May	Napoleon leaves Dresden to join the Grande Armée.
23–24 June	Napoleon's army begins to cross the Niemen, initiating the campaign.
28 June	Napoleon reaches Vilna.

10–11 July	in its withdrawal before the invasion, Barclay's First West Army reaches Drissa.
14 July	Jérôme Bonaparte resigns his command in the Grande Armée in response to criticism of his ineptitude.
19 July	the Tsar leaves the Russian field headquarters.
23 July	Davout blocks Bagration's northward withdrawal in an action at Mohilev.
25–26 July	Murat defeats Russian forces under Ostermann-Tolstoy at Ostrovno.
27–28 July	Napoleon engages Russian forces near Vitebsk and takes the city.
31 July	on Napoleon's left flank, Macdonald takes Dünaburg.
4 August	Barclay and Bagration unite their armies near Smolensk.
8 August	Platov surprises Sebastiani at Inkovo.
13–14 August	Napoleon crosses the Dnieper in an attempt to turn the Russian left.
14 August	Neverovski executes a fighting withdrawal from Krasny.
16 August	Napoleon's vanguard reaches Smolensk.

17 August	Napoleon assaults Smolensk; Russian forces withdraw on the following day.
17–18 August	Oudinot and Gouvion Saint-Cyr check Wittgenstein at Polotsk.
19 August	Napoleon's pursuit after Smolensk is checked at Valutino (or Lubino).
20 August	Kutuzov confirmed in command of Russian forces.
5 September	Napoleon storms and captures the Shevardino Redoubt on the western edge of the Borodino battlefield.
7 September	The battle of Borodino.
9 September	Murat occupies Mozhaisk in pursuit of Kutuzov.
14 September	Napoleon's vanguard reaches Moscow; the city begins to burn that evening.
27 September	Victor reaches Smolensk, providing Napoleon with some support in the rear of the main army.
5 October	Napoleon sends Lauriston in an unsuccessful attempt to negotiate with the Russians.
18 October	Sebastiani surprised at Vinkovo.
18–20 October	Gouvion Saint-Cyr engaged by Wittgenstein at Polotsk and begins to withdraw.
19 October	Napoleon begins the evacuation of Moscow.
24 October	Napoleon's attempted southward manoeuvre blocked at Maloyaroslavets.
3 November	Davout engaged and almost overwhelmed by Miloradovich near Vyazma.
4 November	first heavy snow of the retreat.
9 November	Napoleon reaches Smolensk.
16 November	Chichagov takes the depot at Minsk on his northward march.
17 November	Ney's rearguard quits Smolensk; Napoleon counterattacks Miloradovich near Krasny.
21 November	Chichagov takes Borisov with its crossing over the Berezina.
25–28 November	action at the Berezina as Napoleon's army crosses the river, opposed by Chichagov and Wittgenstein.
29 November	bridges over the Berezina destroyed to hamper Russian pursuit.
5 December	Napoleon quits the army at Smolensk.
9 December	the army reaches Vilna.
11–12 December	remnants of the Grande Armée cross the Niemen at Kovno.
30 December	Treaty of Tauroggen by which the Prussian elements of X Corps proclaim their neutrality, beginning the disintegration of Napoleon's allies.

OPPOSING COMMANDERS

Eugène de Beauharnais (1781–1824), Viceroy of Italy, Napoleon's stepson and one of his most trusted subordinates, commander of IV Corps of the Grande Armée. (Print after Albrecht Adam)

FRENCH COMMANDERS

The problems of scale that prevented Napoleon's personal supervision of important parts of the campaign threw much responsibility onto his senior subordinates, demanding a level of initiative in independent command that some were not used to exercising. Some of the most important are detailed below.

Murat, Marshal Joachim, King of Naples (1767–1815)

Commander of the cavalry of the Grande Armée, Murat owed his position as Grand Duke of Berg (1806–08) and King of Naples (from August 1808) to the patronage of his brother-in-law, Napoleon; but he possessed considerable talents as an inspirational leader of cavalry. Recklessly brave, flamboyant, a superb rider and swordsman who gloried in outrageously theatrical uniforms of his own devising, Murat was the archetypal sabreur who led from the front and attracted widespread admiration both from his own followers and even from the enemy: the Cossacks in particular admired his dash and élan as became evident during the 1812 campaign. As a tactician, Murat was more limited; Napoleon once stated that he was endowed with extraordinary courage but little intelligence, and that he had promoted him beyond his talents. On the battlefield, however, Murat excelled, ever in the forefront of the action, careless of his own safety and an inspiration to those under his command. Despite his reservations, it was to Murat that Napoleon turned over command of what remained of the Grande Armée at the conclusion of the campaign.

Davout, Marshal Louis-Nicolas, duc d'Auerstädt, prince d'Eckmühl (1770–1823)

Arguably the most capable of all Napoleon's subordinates, Davout was a stern disciplinarian with few gracious attributes, hence the nickname 'the Iron Marshal'. He was related to the imperial family, having married the sister of Pauline Bonaparte's husband Leclerc, but his military standing was achieved entirely on merit; he won distinction at Austerlitz, by his victory at Auerstädt, at Eylau and Eckmühl, and his supervision made I Corps the best in the Grande Armée in 1812. Davout was a considerable tactician as well as a brave and determined soldier; more than one witness during the 1812 campaign reported his dissatisfaction with Napoleon over the unimaginative tactics employed on the battlefield: when ordered to make a brutal frontal assault on the Russian line at Borodino he remarked to Louis Lejeune that it

LEFT
Marshal Louis-Nicolas Davout (1770–1823), duc d'Auerstadt and prince d'Eckmühl, arguably Napoleon's most capable lieutenant and commander of I Corps, recognized as the best in the Grande Armée. (Print by Lacoste after Moraine)

CENTRE
Marshal Joachim Murat, King of Naples (1767–1815), Napoleon's brother-in-law and the most flamboyant personality of his age. Brave and admired universally, notably by the Cossacks, he led the Grande Armée's cavalry. (Print by Dean after Delpesch)

RIGHT
Marshal Michel Ney, duc d'Elchingen (1769–1815), commander of III Corps, perhaps best-known by his sobriquet 'bravest of the brave'. (Print by Hall after Gérard)

was a shame he was made to 'take the bull by the horns' rather than attempt a more intelligent manoeuvre.

Ney, Marshal Michel, duc d'Elchingen (1769–1815)

The commander of III Corps in 1812, Ney was the exemplification of a 'fighting general', a man of indomitable spirit that was to win him in 1812 the title 'prince de la Moscowa' and, more famously, the sobriquet 'bravest of the brave'. He was a capable subordinate, distinguished especially at Elchingen (1805), from which he took the title of his dukedom in 1808, but not always the easiest collaborator: his service in the Peninsula had ended when relations with Massena, his superior, broke down irretrievably among accusations of insubordination. Ney was not best suited for independent command but was ideal for leading a corps and following instructions; and, on the battlefield, for his unquenchable spirit and personal courage, as when his force of will held the rearguard together in the darkest period of the 1812 campaign.

Beauharnais, Eugène de, Viceroy of Italy (1781–1824)

Son of Alexandre de Beauharnais, first husband of Empress Josephine, Eugène was Napoleon's stepson and a subordinate commander of unswerving loyalty. Although not a general of the first rank, he displayed considerable military skill as Viceroy of Italy, a post to which he was appointed in 1805. In 1809 he commanded the Army of Italy with some success (though he was assisted by Macdonald), and was distinguished at Wagram. Napoleon trusted his skill sufficiently to assign him a very significant role in the 1812 campaign, leading IV Corps, where he accomplished the tasks allocated to him. Eugène was a popular figure, described as kind, even-tempered and brave, which must have won the trust of his subordinates; his motto 'honour and fidelity' was appropriate.

Poniatowski, Prince Josef (1763–1813)

A member of a distinguished noble family, Poniatowski was probably the most renowned Polish soldier of his age, and a very capable leader of V Corps in the 1812 campaign. He was never a devoted follower of Napoleon, but marched with him through the hope that Napoleon represented the best hope for the creation of a truly independent Polish state. Despite some mistrust of Napoleon, Poniatowski had accepted the post of War Minister in the Duchy of Warsaw, and subsequently the head of its army, in 1807, and his reforms produced an excellent army despite the financial strictures under which he had to work. Napoleon recognized potential problems arising from Poniatowski's national aspirations and hero status among the Poles, but he served with distinction in the 1812 campaign and was entrusted with leading the right wing at Borodino. Despite misgivings Poniatowski remained loyal to Napoleon and was appointed a marshal on 15 October 1813, shortly before he was drowned crossing the Elster at Leipzig.

Oudinot, Marshal Nicolas-Charles, duc de Reggio (1767–1847)

Commander of II Corps, in which role he was considerably distinguished in the 1812 campaign, protecting Napoleon's northern flank, and in the fight to permit the escape of the Grande Armée at the Berezina, Oudinot was distinguished more for his courage and determination than for military genius. He was probably the most frequently wounded of all senior commanders of the period – he had to relinquish his command temporarily during the 1812 campaign to recuperate from another injury – yet nothing seemed to deter him from his duty; he once remarked to Napoleon that he had never had time to be frightened. Napoleon admitted that Oudinot was not especially bright, but he was a good organizer and, as Massena remarked, was ideally suited as a second-in-command.

Bonaparte, Jérôme, King of Westphalia (1784–1860)

The youngest and least talented of Napoleon's brothers, Jérôme was appointed to the throne of Westphalia by Napoleon, but was not a success; his extravagant lifestyle did nothing for that state's parlous economy and he showed no military talent. So lethargic was his handling of VIII Corps in the first stage of the 1812 campaign that he went home in a sulk following Napoleon's criticism, and although subsequently reconciled demonstrated no improvement in his abilities as a general at Waterloo.

Junot, General Jean-Andoche, duc d'Abrantès (1771–1813)

An old companion of Napoleon, who he had served as an aide in Italy, Junot was appointed to command VIII Corps after Jérôme Bonaparte's departure.

LEFT
Prince Josef Anton Poniatowski (1763–1813), commander of the Polish V Corps of the Grande Armée, that held the right wing at Borodino. He was appointed as a Marshal of France three days before his death at the battle of Leipzig in October 1813. (Print by Lacoste)

RIGHT
General Jean-Andoche Junot, duc d'Abrantès (1771–1813), an old companion-in-arms of Napoleon who succeeded Jérôme Bonaparte as commander of VIII Corps but proved no more successful. (Engraving by T. Beard)

His previous military record had been mixed: he enjoyed some success in leading the invasion of Portugal (from where he took his ducal title) but had been defeated at Vimeiro and achieved little greater success subsequently in the Peninsula, including being shot in the nose in a skirmish. Known for a chaotic and dissipated lifestyle – it is likely that syphilis contributed to the mental derangement that led to his suicide in 1813 – Junot performed little better than his predecessor Jérôme in 1812, and was criticized severely for mishandling the intended entrapment of the enemy during the Russian withdrawal from Smolensk.

THE TSAR'S GENERALS

Relations within the Russian command were troubled, beset with rivalries and mistrust, though it included a number of very distinguished and capable officers, some of whom are listed below.

Barclay de Tolly, General of Infantry Mikhail Andreas (1761–1818)
The principal Russian commander in the first stage of the 1812 campaign, Barclay de Tolly laboured under a considerable disadvantage. Despite a long and distinguished service in the Russian army, he was regarded as a foreigner by the 'old' Russian heirarchy which tended to blame such individuals for any failings in the military system. This was unfair: despite his distant Scots ancestry, Barclay was a loyal and capable servant of the Tsar. He had been appointed Minister of War in 1810 and had instituted importantly beneficial reforms to the Russian military, but contemporary opinion did not mark him in the first rank of field commanders. The general perception was that Barclay was a man of calculation rather than instinct; Carl von Clausewitz, who served on the Russian staff during the campaign, thought him 'a rather cold man, not very susceptible of suggestions', while the French general Philippe-Paul de Ségur, author of one of the earliest histories of the campaign (in which he

LEFT
General Mikhail Andreas Barclay de Tolly (1761–1818), Russian Minister of War and commander of First West Army. (Print after St Aubin)

RIGHT
General Peter Bagration (1765–1812), commander of Second West Army and the most senior commander to suffer a mortal wound at Borodino. (Print after Cardelli)

served) wrote of the 'cool valour, the scientific, methodical, and tenacious genius of Barclay, whose mind, German like his birth [sic], was for calculating every thing'. Although not among the greatest of commanders, Barclay behaved with noted courage in 1812 and while his conduct prior to Borodino was criticized for lack of resolution, his refusal to engage Napoleon early in the campaign prevented the Russian forces from being destroyed piecemeal.

Bagration, General of Infantry Peter Ivanovich (1765–1812)

Bagration was a general admired universally throughout the Russian military; indeed, there was a pun on his name that produced the term 'God of the Army'. Descended from Georgian nobility, he had served long and with distinction in the Russian army, serving under the great hero Suvarov in Italy and Switzerland, and to many he seemed to be Suvarov's heir, a regard that cannot have helped the acceptance of Barclay as the senior commander, and relations between the two were distinctly strained. Bagration had won plaudits for a number of campaigns in which he had been distinguished, including Austerlitz, Eylau, Friedland and against the Turks, and Robert Wilson wrote of his merits, 'eyes flashing with Asiatic fire. Gentle, gracious, chivalrously brave, he was beloved by everyone, and admired by all who witnessed his exploits. No officer ever excelled him in the direction of an advance or rear guard.'[2] Ségur thought him the antithesis of Barclay, representing the 'martial, bold, and vehement instinct' of Suvarov; 'terrible in battle, but acquainted with no other book than nature, no other instructor than memory, no other counsels than his own inspirations', and one who 'trembled with shame at the idea of retreating without fighting'[3]. Robert Ker Porter regarded him as 'an honour to human nature', but the emphasis on his personal qualities and the loyalty they engendered should not conceal his considerable technical military skills.

Kutuzov, General of Infantry Mikhail Larionovich (1745–1813)

Kutuzov came late to the 1812 campaign, and was appointed to chief command out of necessity, as will be explained in the account of the campaign that follows. Unlike many Russian officers, he was not only experienced in terms of campaign service but was unusually well educated: he could speak French, German, Polish, Swedish, English and Turkish as well as his native tongue. His military career had included much active service in Poland and against the Ottoman Empire, notably as Governor-General of the Crimea (1787) and in the 1788–91 Turkish War. Within the army he was popular and admired, and was viewed by many as another heir to Suvarov, but this popularity did not extend to the Tsar and his advisors, leading to administrative duties after the Austerlitz campaign, though he was not responsible for that disaster. His role in 1812 was more strategical than tactical, and as will be noted, he did little at Borodino, not helped by his state of health and immobility, beyond establishing the course of action that led to the army fighting there; yet his role in determining the outcome of the campaign, and in raising the morale of the army, was crucial.

Wittgenstein, General Ludwig Adolf Peter (1769–1843)

During the 1812 campaign Wittgenstein enjoyed an element of independent command not available to many Russian subordinate commanders, despite his I Corps forming part of Barclay's First West Army. Wittgenstein was another of the 'foreigners' in Russian service; his family was of Westphalian

origin, but his father had settled in Russia and Wittgenstein followed him into the Russian army. He had served in Poland in 1794–95, in the Caucasus and as a general officer in Bagration's advance guard at Austerlitz. He performed well enough in 1812 to succeed Kutuzov in command of the Russian and Prussian forces, but after reverses and criticism in 1813 reverted to command of a corps and was replaced by Barclay. Wounded severely at Bar-sur-Aube, he rose to the rank of field-marshal and in 1834 was awarded the title of Prince of Sayn–Wittgenstein–Ludwigsberg by the King of Prussia.

Platov, General Matvei Ivanovich (1751–1818)
Famous beyond the borders of his own country as the representative of the colourful (and to western European eyes somewhat mysterious) Cossacks, Platov had served with distinction under Suvarov and had survived a period of disgrace and exile during the reign of Tsar Paul I, to took the field against Napoleon in 1807–07 and against the Turks. He became Hetman (leader or commander) of the Don Cossacks in 1801, and was at their head when their value as raiders and skirmishers was confirmed during the 1812 campaign. It was at his suggestion that the wide and influential cavalry flanking manoeuvre was executed on the Russian right at Borodino. Extremely popular among his own troops, Platov was feted elsewhere in Europe after the war.

Chichagov, Admiral Pavel (1767–1849)
Originally a naval officer, Chichagov had commanded the Russian squadron that cooperated with the British during the Netherlands expedition of 1799, and had served as Navy Minister from 1808 to 1812. In the latter year he was appointed to command the Army of the Danube (or Moldavia) and led the southern arm of the 'pincer' that attempted to block Napoleon's escape from Russia. He was not, perhaps, an obvious choice; his subordinate General Louis-Alexandre Langeron (a French aristocrat in Russian service) stated that his knowledge of military matters was limited, that he was prone to devising impractical plans and unwilling to take advice, but was so honest that he

tended to despise his own nation for the corruption he perceived as common. His inexperience was perhaps demonstrated by his surprise at Borisov and in being deceived by Oudinot's feint at the beginning of the Berezina action. A noted anglophile, he had been raised in England, married an English wife and subsequently became a British subject.

Miloradovich, General Mikhail Andreivich (1770–1825)

Miloradovich did not command a corps in 1812 but was assigned greater responsibility, having authority over the right wing at Borodino. He was an officer of wide experience, having served against the Turks and in Poland, and as joint commander of the allied 4th Column at Austerlitz. Eugen of Württemberg knew him well and left an appealing account of his character, describing him as a knight of the purest sense, fearlessly brave, even-tempered, with a ready wit that never left him even in battle, and unfailingly calm and courteous under the most trying of circumstances. This extended to his style of command: always in the forefront of the action, he would tell the commander on the spot to continue to act as he saw fit and to regard himself merely as a guest; not a superior. He helped lead the pursuit after the evacuation of Moscow, and was further distinguished in 1813–14. As Governor of St Petersburg he attempted to talk to the leaders of the Decembrist revolt in 1825 but was shot in the back and killed.

Raevski, General Nikolai Nikolaievich (1771–1829)

Although one of the lesser-ranking Russian commanders, leading VII Corps in the 1812 campaign, Raevski was especially distinguished in the operations around Smolensk and in the defence of the Great Redoubt at Borodino, which is sometimes known by his name, the Raevski Redoubt. He had seen extensive service, against the Ottoman Empire, Poland, against Napoleon in 1806–09 and Sweden in 1809, and was clearly a most determined individual. Shortly before Borodino he was accidentally injured in the leg by a bayonet, but remained with his command despite, due to his immobility, having to station himself within the Redoubt and thus in great danger. By his own account the smoke became so thick that he was unable to see the enemy until they actually poured into the Redoubt. Shortly before that he had declined to take over command of the Russian left after Bagration was wounded, believing that his duty was to maintain the position originally assigned to him. He served subsequently in the campaigns of 1813–14.

Neverovski, General Dmitri Petrovich (1771–1813)

Although he held only a divisional command – the 27th – Neverovski gained great distinction in the operations leading up to, and in the battle of, Borodino. In 1804 he had commanded a regiment of marines and subsequently the distinguished Pavlov Grenadiers, but it was his fighting retreat with the 27th Division near Krasny that first won him great renown, which was enhanced by his stubborn defence of the *flèches* at Borodino. He continued to lead the 27th Division and was killed at Leipzig; his burial at Borodino, in the region of his fight there, was appropriate.

2 Wilson, Sir Robert, *Brief Remarks on the Character and Composition of the Russian Army*, London 1810, p. 156.
3 Ségur, P. de, *History of the Expedition to Russia undertaken by the Emperor Napoleon in the Year 1812*, London, 1825, Vol. I p. 226.

OPPOSING PLANS AND FORCES

NAPOLEON'S PLANS

The operation Napoleon planned was on a scale never before contemplated, and he had no illusions about the size of the undertaking: he was aware of the nature of the Russian forces, the huge extent of the region of operations, and of the dearth of resources. The army he organized was as much as three times as great as any he had led before, truly meriting the name 'La Grande Armée', and requiring a system of control and logistics more complex than anything known previously. Supplies and munitions had been gathered in key German and Polish fortresses from as early as 1810, ostensibly as a safeguard against any supposed Russian aggression, but the process accelerated in 1811 when Napoleon decided he must initiate hostilities. He strengthened his own army over this period, and withdrew experienced formations from the Iberian Peninsula, from where they could ill be spared. He also demanded contributions from his allied or client states, producing not only the largest but most nationally diverse force that he had ever commanded.

LEFT
French chasseur à cheval, the category of regiment that made up the larger part of the light cavalry. (Print after Hippolyte Bellangé)

RIGHT
Dress uniform of the Fusiliers-Grenadiers of Napoleon's Imperial Guard, a regiment that served in the 2nd Division of the Guard in the 1812 campaign. (Print by Guichon after Hippolyte Bellangé)

LEFT
A universal campaign modification of infantry uniform: a Fusilier-Grenadier of the Imperial Guard: for campaigning loose trousers were usually worn and the shako-ornaments removed. (Print after Vilain)

RIGHT
Napoleon's Imperial Guard: an officer of Chasseurs à Pied (left) and a Fusilier-Chasseur in campaign dress. (Print by Lacoste after Vernier)

Napoleon's planned field of operations stretched from the Baltic coast to the southern extent of the Russo-Polish frontier, and he organized his forces accordingly. For his first line, the principal striking force, he created what were in effect 'army groups', though not titled as such. Under his own command was a force that comprised three corps d'armée, numbered I–III, two corps of 'reserve cavalry' and his own Imperial Guard.

The Guard comprised three infantry divisions, under Marshals Lefebvre and Mortier, and the Guard cavalry of Marshal Bessières, about 47,000 strong and almost entirely French in composition. I Corps, alongside the Guard perhaps the most elite of the army and some 72,000 strong, was led by Marshal Louis-Nicolas Davout. II Corps, about 37,000 strong, was commanded by Marshal Nicolas-Charles Oudinot, duc de Reggio. III Corps, 39,000 in number, was led by Marshal Michel Ney, duc d'Elchingen. Though predominantly French, half his cavalry and one of his three infantry divisions were from Württemberg.

Napoleon's cavalry was under the overall control of his brother-in-law, Joachim Murat, King of Naples. Part of Napoleon's main army group were two corps of 'reserve cavalry' (i.e. self-contained formations, not attached to an infantry formation); I Cavalry Corps, about 12,000 in number, was led by General Etienne-Marie Nansouty, an aristocrat acknowledged as one of the best leaders of heavy cavalry, while II Cavalry Corps, about 10,500 strong, was commanded by General Louis-Pierre Montbrun, a man described as from the same mould as Murat. The nucleus of both corps were French cuirassiers, with light cavalry that included some Polish regiments.

To support his own force, Napoleon organized two further contingents, the first being the Army of Italy, led by Eugène de Beauharnais, Viceroy of Italy. He led his own IV Corps, about 46,000 strong, of mixed French and Italian composition. VI Corps, about 25,000 strong, was led by General Laurent Gouvion Saint-Cyr (appointed a marshal in August), an able general but a seemingly morose and introverted man whose relations with Napoleon

LEFT
A fusilier of French line infantry. Some regiments in the campaign wore the new, 1812-regulation coatee, but others retained the earlier long-tailed coat shown here.

RIGHT
French infantry: a drummer and sapeur (pioneer). (Print after Phippoteaux)

BELOW LEFT
Foreign regiments that served in the French army: a sapeur of the Polish Vistula Legion that was attached to the Imperial Guard during the campaign (left), and a grenadier of the Portuguese Legion, two regiments of which served with II Corps and one in Ney's III Corps.

BELOW CENTRE
Württemberg infantry and light infantry (right); this state provided Marchand's 25th Division of III Corps, heavily engaged at Borodino. (Print after Charles Rozat de Mandres)

BELOW RIGHT
The small contingent from Baden was among the best elements of the Grande Armée, serving in IX Corps: private (left) and officer of infantry. (Print after Charles Rozat de Mandres)

were characterized by mutual distrust. His troops were all Bavarian. Eugène also had under his command III Cavalry Corps, largely French and almost 10,000 strong, led by General Emmanuel Grouchy.

The second of the supporting armies was led by Napoleon's brother Jérôme, King of Westphalia. His own VIII Corps, about 18,000 strong, was entirely Westphalian. Also under his command was V Corps, some 36,000 strong, all Polish, commanded by Prince Josef Poniatowski; and VII Corps, entirely Saxon, some 17,000 strong, led by the Swiss general Jean-Louis Reynier. Also with Jérôme was IV Cavalry Corps, about 8,000 strong anf consisting of Polish, Saxon and Westphalian troops, led by General Marie-Victor Latour-Maubourg.

A number of formations were in reserve, intended initially to serve as a source of reinforcement for the corps in the front line. Principal of these was IX Corps led by Marshal Claude Victor, duc de Bellune, about 33,000 strong, partially French, partially Polish, and with contingents from Berg, Baden, Hesse-Darmstadt and Saxony. XI Corps, commanded by the veteran Marshal Pierre-Francois Augereau, occupied the rear areas in a number of detachments, approximately 50,000 strong. Two additional forces operated on the flanks of Napoleon's front line. In the north, on the left flank, X Corps under Marshal Jacques-Etienne Macdonald, duc de Tarente, was about 32,000 strong, half Prussians and the remainder Polish, Bavarian and Westphalian; and on the right or southern flank was the Austrian Reserve Corps of Prince Karl Philipp Schwarzenberg, about 34,000 strong.

Despite its enormous size, the quality of Napoleon's army was far from uniform. Alongside the reliable and experienced elements such as the regiments of the Imperial Guard and those battle-hardened in previous campaigns (although apart from the units recently withdrawn from Spain, the last major campaign had been three years earlier), there were other formations of less impressive quality. Among the allied contingents were some of high repute – the small Baden army, for example, was of noted mettle and has been described as the best of the German contingents – but others were notably unenthusiastic.

Alongside mixed quality there was also the problem of scale. Napoleon maintained perhaps the most sophisticated headquarters system of any at the time, encompassing command, intelligence and logistics, in which his chief of staff, Marshal Louis-Alexandre Berthier, prince de Neuchâtel, was an invaluable assistant; but the forces involved were so large, and the distances so enormous, that it was impossible for him to supervise all operations in person. The fact that few of Napoleon's subordinates had ever been allowed to exercise initiative in independent command compounded the problems of scale, which also impacted upon the provision of supplies. The practice of foraging or 'living off the land', as utilized by French armies early in the period, had proved not to work adequately, so a system of supply depots and transportation of unsurpassed sophistication had been created; as Napoleon had stated earlier in 1812, they should expect nothing from the countryside but would have to take everything with them. The problem, however, was not only one of scale, but was complicated by the poor state of the roads leading into Russia, which presented severe difficulties for the heavier transport wagons; so that despite the immense logistical organization instituted by Napoleon, it was to prove entirely insufficient when subjected to the stresses of the 1812 campaign.

Napoleon's claim that he sought no territorial acquisition was true: he never intended a war of conquest, but as in previous campaigns intended to destroy the enemy's field army, and so compel the Tsar to make peace upon French terms. He was aware of previous attempts against Russia: in 1610 Sigismund III of Poland had captured Moscow, but had his garrison massacred in 1612, and an invasion of Russia had caused the ruin of Charles XII of Sweden in 1709; but Napoleon planned to use overwhelming force to bring about a swift victory.

THE TSAR'S RESOURCES

Opposing the Grande Armée was a military establishment in some respects different from any other. The Russian army was recruited by conscription for

LEFT
Officer of Russian Guard
infantry in the 1812-regulation
uniform, including the
distinctive concave-topped
shako. (Print by Jacquemin)

CENTRE
Officer of Russian hussars.
(Print by Goddard & Booth)

RIGHT
Officer of Russian horse
artillery, wearing the tall,
crested, heavy cavalry-style
helmet. (Print by Goddard
& Booth)

a period of 25 years' service, from a numerous population of which more than half were serfs bound to agricultural estates, little more than slaves. Despite the deprivation from which they came, and conditions equally harsh in the army, the Russian soldiery was renowned for astonishing stoicism and resilience, with a devotion to Tsar, religion and homeland that caused observers to marvel. The British officer Sir Robert Wilson, who observed them at first hand, is often quoted in his expression of admiration, but equally illuminating is the opinion of an enemy. The French cavalryman Jean-Baptiste de Marbot recounted an incident at Golymin in 1807 in which the Russians,

> knowing that Marshal Lannes was marching to cut off their retreat by capturing Pultusk, three leagues farther on… were trying to reach that point before him at any price. Therefore, although our soldiers fired upon them at 25 paces, they continued their march without replying, because in order to do so they would have had to halt, and every moment was precious. So every division, every regiment, filed past, without saying a word or slackening its pace for a moment. The streets were filled with dying and wounded, but not a groan was to be heard, for they were forbidden. You might have said that we were firing upon shadows. At last our soldiers charged the Russian soldiers with the bayonet, and only when they pierced them could they be convinced that they were dealing with men.
> Marbot, J. B. A. M., *The Memoirs of Baron de Marbot*, trans. A. J. Butler, London 1913, Vol. I p. 200.

Wilson wrote of their resilience not just in combat: 'inured to the extremes of weather and hardship; to the worst and scantiest food; to marches for days and nights… obstinately brave… devoted to their sovereign, their chief, and their country. Religious without being weakened by superstition; patient, docile and obedient; possessing all the energetic characteristics of a barbarian people, with the advantages engrafted by civilization.' Recalling the eve of Eylau, he described 'the desolating misery of a night passed without food, without any moisture to quench drought but iced snow, without any shelter,

without any covering but the rags of their garments, with bare and wounded feet, without fuel, without any consolation, and sleep interrupted by the groans of the dying, or preparations for action, not all this complicated bitterness of condition could humble the spirit or weaken the ardour of this illustrious host'[4]. Such characteristics were an important consideration in the forthcoming campaign.

Conversely, the Russian officer corps was regarded as among the worst in Europe: recruited largely from the minor gentry, many had little opportunity for advancement and thus limited incentive for perfecting their trade. Such factors led to the employment of a considerable number of foreign officers, many of whom attained high rank and whose presence was sometimes the cause of friction within the army. (Not all so-called 'foreigners' were new arrivals: there had been a tradition of employing foreign professionals for generations, and thus the most prominent of them in 1812, Mikhail Barclay

de Tolly, though of Scottish-Livonian stock, came from a family settled in the Baltic region in the 17th century.)

The Russian army possessed one resource unique in Europe: large numbers of irregular light cavalry. The most important of these were the Cossacks, renowned for courage, hardiness, a lack of military discipline and a penchant for looting. They were generally not very effective in a conventional battle; as Wilson described, 'it must not be supposed that they are calculated to act generally in line. Their service is of a different character, which requires a greater latitude and liberty of operation. They act in dispersion, and when they do re-unite to charge, it is not with a systematic formation, but en masse.'[5] As skirmishers and raiders, however, they were unsurpassed, and their reputation engendered dread among their enemies; as Wilson phrased it, 'Terror preceded [their] charge'. Such attributes would play an important role in the 1812 campaign. Their leader was General Matvei Platov, who had become Hetman (chief) of the Don Cossacks in 1801, and who from his association with them became one of the best-known Russian commanders.

Much less effective were the hordes of undisciplined Asiatic light horse, generally styled Bashkirs and Calmucks, some of whom were armed with bows and arrows. They were generally regarded with much less fear than were the Cossacks, as demonstrated by the nickname bestowed by the French, '*cupidons du nord*' – 'northern cupids' – from their archaic weapons.

To oppose Napoleon's anticipated invasion, the Tsar organized two principal forces covering the border over which the enemy would advance. Along the north of the front was the First West Army, about 127,000 strong, commanded by General Mikhail Barclay de Tolly. The southern sector of the front was covered by Second West Army, 48,000 strong or more, led by General Peter Bagration. Covering the Russian left flank, south of the Pripet marshes, was the Third West Army of General Alexander Tormasov, in course of assembling, about 45,000 strong, while other forces included Admiral Pavel Chichagov's Army of the Danube, about 35,000 in number, marching north. In addition to the regular forces there was a militia or '*opolchenie*'. There had been fears of arming the peasantry, notably in recollection of Pugachev's 'serf revolt' of 1773, but a brief experiment had organized militia in 1806–07 and more than 220,000 men were enrolled during 1812. Training and equipment was generally rudimentary but the force represented an important expression of national determination, and during the campaign some militiamen received considerable praise. Wilson, for example, recorded how at Maloyaroslavets 'the very militia who had just joined (and who, being armed only with pikes, formed a third rank to the battalions) not only stood as steady under the cannonade as their veteran comrades, but charged the sallying enemy with as ardent ferocity,'[6] while Wittgenstein commended the St Petersburg corps who 'have fought with such good will and courage that they could not be exceeded by their comrades, the old soldiers, and they have distinguished themselves, in particular manner in columns, with the bayonet.'[7]

4. Wilson, *Brief Remarks*, pp. 1, 3–4.
5. ibid. p. 29.
6 Wilson, Sir Robert, *Narrative of Events during the Invasion of Russia by Napoleon Bonaparte*, London, 1860, p. 225.
7. Translation from *Edinburgh Evening Courant*, 14 November 1812.

ORDERS OF BATTLE

Some differences in brigading are recorded in various sources, usually the result of reorganizations and changes of personnel during the campaign. For example, General Jacques (or Joseph) Ferrière is sometimes stated as leading the 12th Light Cavalry Brigade in Eugène's IV Corps at Borodino; but in July he had been appointed governor of the province of Bialystock, and had been replaced by General Claude-Raymond Guyon. Similarly, General Horace-François-Bastien Sébastiani is sometimes listed as commanding the 2nd Light Cavalry Division, but on 9 August he had been replaced by General Claude-Pierre Pajol, who earlier in the campaign had led a light cavalry brigade in Davout's I Corps. This example is complicated further by the fact that Sébastiani was appointed to lead II Cavalry Corps following Montbrun's death at Borodino.

GRANDE ARMÉE AT BORODINO
(Emperor Napoleon I)

Note: infantry regiments consisted of four battalions, and cavalry regiments of four squadrons, unless a different number is stated in parentheses. Units were part of the French army (even if composed of foreigners) unless stated otherwise. It was usual to identify brigades by the name of their commander.

HEADQUARTERS (chief of staff Marshal Louis-Alexandre Berthier)
Gendarmerie d'Elite (2 sq), 7th Chasseurs à Cheval, 2nd Hessian Regt. (1)

IMPERIAL GUARD
Old Guard (Marshal François-Joseph Lefebvre)
1st Div (Delaborde):
    Bde Berthèzene: 4th Tirailleurs, 4th & 5th Voltigeurs (2 each)
    Bde Lanusse: 5th & 6th Tirailleurs, 6th Voltigeurs (2 each)
3rd Division (Curial):
    Bde Boyer: 1st & 2nd Chasseurs à Pied, 1st–3rd Grenadiers à Pied (2 each)

Young Guard (Marshal Edouard-Adolphe Mortier)
Division Roguet:
    Bde Lanabère: 1st Voltigeurs, 1st Tirailleurs (2 each)
    Bde Boyledieu: Fusiliers-Chasseurs, Fusiliers-Grenadiers (2 each)

Vistula Legion (Claparède)
    Bde Chlopicki: 1st & 2nd Regts. (3 each)
    Bde Bronikowski: 3rd & 4th Regts. (3 each)

Guard Cavalry (Marshal Jean-Baptiste Bessières)
    1st Bde (Saint-Sulpice): Dragoons, Grenadiers à Cheval
    2nd Bde (Guyot): Chasseurs à Cheval, Mamelukes (1)
    3rd Bde (Colbert): 1st & 2nd Lancers

Attached
Chasseurs à Cheval of the Portuguese Legion (3), 28th Chasseurs à Cheval (1), Velites of Prince Borghese, Velites of the Tuscan Guard (1 bn each), 2nd Baden Regt. (2)

I CORPS (Marshal Louis-Nicolas Davout)
1st Division (Morand)
    Bde Dalton: 13th Light (5)
    Bde Gratien: 17th Line (5)
    Bde Bonnamy: 30th Line (5)

2nd Division (Friant)
  Bde Dufour: 15th Light (5)
  Bde Van Dedem: 33rd Line (5)
  Bde Grandeau: 48th Line (5), Regt. Joseph-Napoleon (Spanish) (2)
3rd Division (Gérard)
  Bde Gérard: 7th Light (5)
  Bde Desailly: 12th Line (5)
  Bde Leclerc: 21st Line (5), 127th Line (2)
4th Division (Dessaix)
  Bde Friedrichs: 85th Line (5)
  Bde Leguay: 108th Line (5)
5th Division (Compans)
  Bde Duppelin: 25th Line (5)
  Bde Teste: 57th Line (5)
  Bde Guyardet: 61st Line (5)
  Bde Lonchamp: 111th Line (5)
Corps Cavalry (Giradin)
  1st Light Bde (Girardin): 2nd Chasseurs à Cheval, 9th Polish Lancers
  2nd Light Bde (Bordessoule): 1st & 3rd Chasseurs à Cheval

III CORPS (Marshal Michel Ney)

10th Division (Ledru)
  Bde Gengoult: 24th Light, 4th Regt. Portuguese Legion (2)
  Bde Marion: 46th Line
  Bde Bruny: 72nd Line
11th Division (Razout)
  Bde Joubert: 4th Line
  Bde Compère: 18th Line, 2nd Regt. Portuguese Legion (2)
  Bde D'Henin: 93rd Line
25th (Württemberg) Division (Marchand)
  Bde von Hügel: 1st & 4th Württemberg Regts. (2 each)
  Bde von Koch: 2nd & 6th Württemberg Regts. (2 each)
  Bde von Brüsselle: 1st & 2nd Württemberg Jägers (1 each), 1st & 2nd Württemberg Light Infantry (1 each)
Corps Cavalry
  9th Light Cavalry Bde (Mourier): 11th Hussars, 6th Chevau-Légers-Lanciers, 4th Württemberg Mounted Jägers
  14th Light Cavalry Bde (Beurmann): 4th Chasseurs à Cheval, 1st & 2nd Württemberg Chevauxlegers

IV CORPS (Eugène de Beauharnais, Viceroy of Italy)

Italian Guard
  Infantry (Lecchi): Velites, Guard Infantry, Guard Conscripts (2 each)
  Cavalry (Triaire): Guards of Honour (1), Guard & Queen's Dragoons
13th Division (Delzons)
  Bde Huard: 8th Light (2), 84th Line, 1st Croatian Regt. (2)
  Bde Plauzonne: 92nd & 104th Line
14th Division (Broussier)
  Bde de Sivray: 18th Light (2), 9th Line
  Bde Almeras: 35th Line, Regt. Joseph-Napoleon (Spanish) (2)
  Bde Pastol (who was absent, ill): 53rd Line
Corps Cavalry (Ornano)
  12th Light Cavalry Bde (Guyon): 9th & 13th Chasseurs à Cheval
  13th Light Cavalry Bde (Villata): 2nd & 3rd Italian Chasseurs à Cheval
  21st Light Cavalry Bde (Seydewitz): 3rd & 6th Bavarian Chevauxlegers
  22nd Light Cavalry Bde (Preysing): 4th & 5th Bavarian Chevauxlegers

V CORPS (Prince Josef Poniatowski)

16th Division (Zayonczek)
  Bde Mielzynski: 3rd & 15th Polish Line (3 each)
  Bde Poszhowski: 16th Polish Line (3)
18th Division (Kniaziewicz)
  Bde Grabowski: 2nd & 8th Polish Line (3 each)
  Bde Wierzbinski: 12th Polish Line (3)
Corps Cavalry
  18th Light Cavalry Bde (Niemoiewski): 1st Polish Chasseurs à Cheval, 12th Polish Lancers
  19th Light Cavalry Bde (Tyskiewicz): 4th Polish Chasseurs à Cheval
  20th Light Cavalry Bde (Sulkowski): 5th Polish Chasseurs à Cheval, 13th Polish Lancers

VIII CORPS (General Jean-Andoche Junot)

23rd (Westphalian) Division (Tharreau)
  Bde Damas: 3rd Light Bn, 2nd & 6th Line (2 each)
  Bde Wickenberg: 2nd Light Bn, 3rd (2) & 7th Line (3)
24th (Westphalian) Division (Ochs)
  Bde Legras: Jäger-Carabiniers, Guard Jägers, Guard Grenadiers, 1st Light Bn (1 each)
Corps Cavalry
  24th (Westphalian) Light Cavalry Bde (von Hammerstein): 1st & 2nd Hussars
  Bde Wolf: Westphalian Guard Chevauxlegers

I CAVALRY CORPS (General Etienne-Marie Nansouty)

1st Light Cavalry Division (Bruyères)
  3rd Light Cavalry Bde (Jacquinot): 7th Hussars, 9th Chevau-Légers-Lanciers
  4th Light Cavalry Bde (Piré): 8th Hussars, 16th Chasseurs à Cheval
  15th Light Cavalry Bde (Roussel d'Hurbal): 6th & 8th Polish Lancers, 2nd Prussian Hussars
1st Cuirassier Division (Saint-Germain)
  1st Bde (Bessières): 2nd Cuirassiers
  2nd Bde (Bruno): 3rd Cuirassiers
  3rd Bde (Queunot): 9th Cuirassiers, 1st Chevau-Légers-Lanciers
5th Cuirassier Division (Valence)
  1st Bde (Reynaud): 6th Cuirassiers
  2nd Bde (Dejean): 11th Cuirassiers
  3rd Bde (Delagrange): 12th Cuirassiers, 5th Chevau-Légers-Lanciers

II CAVALRY CORPS (General Louis-Pierre Montbrun)

2nd Light Cavalry Division (Pajol)
  7th Light Cavalry Bde (Saint-Génies): 11th & 12th Chasseurs à Cheval
  8th Light Cavalry Bde (Baurth): 5th & 9th Hussars
  16th Light Cavalry Bde (Subervie): 1st Prussian Uhlans, 3rd Württemberg Mounted Jägers, 10th Polish Hussars
2nd Cuirassier Division (Watier de St. Alphonse)
  1st Bde (Beaumont): 5th Cuirassiers
  2nd Bde (Dornes): 8th Cuirassiers
  3rd Bde (Richter): 10th Cuirassiers, 2nd Chevau-Légers-Lanciers
4th Cuirassier Division (Defrance)
  1st Bde (Bouvier des Eclaz): 1st Carabiniers
  2nd Bde (Chouard): 2nd Carabiniers
  3rd Bde (Paultre de la Motte): 1st Cuirassiers, 4th Chevau-Légers-Lanciers

III CAVALRY CORPS (General Emmanuel Grouchy)

3rd Light Cavalry Division (Chastel)
- 10th Light Cavalry Bde (Gauthrin): 6th Hussars, 8th Chasseurs à cheval
- 11th Light Cavalry Bde (Gérard): 6th & 25th Chasseurs à Cheval
- 17th Light Cavalry Bde (Dommanget): 1st & 2nd Bavarian Chevauxlegers
- Saxon Chevauxlegers 'Prince Albrecht'

6th Heavy Cavalry Division (Houssaye)
- 1st Bde (Thiry): 7th & 23rd Dragoons
- 2nd Bde (Seron): 28th & 30th Dragoons

IV CAVALRY CORPS (GENERAL MARIE-VICTOR LATOUR-MAUBOURG)

4th Light Cavalry Division (Rozniecki)
- 29th Light Cavalry Bde (Turno): 3rd, 11th (3) & 16th Polish Lancers

7th Cuirassier Division (Lorge)
- 1st Bde (Thielemann): Saxon Garde du Corps and Zastrow Cuirassiers, 14th Polish Cuirassiers
- 2nd Bde (Lepel): 1st & 2nd Westphalian Cuirassiers

Noted below are those elements of the Grande Armée not included in the Borodino order of battle; unless stated otherwise in parentheses, infantry regiments had four battalions and cavalry regiments four squadrons.

II CORPS (Marshal Nicolas-Charles Oudinot)

6th Division (Legrand)
- Bde Albert: 26th Light
- Bde Maison: 19th Line
- Bde Moreau: 56th Line
- Bde Pamplona: l28th Line, 3rd Regt. Portuguese Legion (2 each)

8th Division (Verdier)
- Bde Viviès: 11th Light, 2nd Line (5)
- Bde Pouget: 37th Line, l24th Line (3)

9th Division (Merle)
- Bde Amey: 4th Swiss Regt (3), 3rd Croatian Regt. (2)
- Bde Candras: 1st Swiss Regt. (2), 2nd Swiss Regt. (3)
- Bde Coutard: l23rd Line, 3rd Swiss Regt. (3)

Corps Cavalry
- 5th Light Bde (Castex): 23rd & 24th Chasseurs à Cheval
- 6th Light Bde (Corbineau): 7th & 20th Chasseurs à Cheval, 8th Chevau-Légers-Lanciers

III CORPS (Marshal Michel Ney)

25th (Württemberg) Division: 7th Württemberg Regt. joined in November

V CORPS (Prince Josef Poniatowski)

17th Division (Dombrowski):
- Bde Zoltowski: 1st & 6th Polish Regts. (3 each)
- Bde Pakosz: 14th & 17th Polish Regts. (3 each)

VI CORPS (General Laurent Gouvion Saint-Cyr; Marshal from 27 August 1812)

19th (Bavarian) Division (Deroy)
- Bde Siebein: 1st & 9th Line (2 each), 1st Light Bn
- Bde Raglowich: 4th & 10th Line (2 each), 3rd Light Bn
- Bde Rechberg: 8th Line (2), 6th Light Bn

20th (Bavarian) Division (Wrede)
- Bde Vincenti: 2nd & 6th Line (2 each), 2nd Light Bn
- Bde Beckers: 3rd & 7th Line, 4th Light Bn

- Bde Habermann, subsequently Scherer: 5th & 11th Line, 5th Light Bn Corps Cavalry: Chevauxlegers attached to IV Corps

VII CORPS (General Jean-Louis Reynier)

21st (Saxon) Division (Lecoq)
- Bde Steindel: Regts. Prinz Friedrich & Prinz Clemens (2 each), Liebenau Grenadier Bn
- Bde Nostitz: Regt. Prinz Anton, 2nd Light Infantry (2 each)

22nd (Saxon) Division (Gutschmid, subsequently Funck)
- Bde v. Sahr: 2nd Light Infantry (2), Grenadier Bns v. Anger & v. Spiegel
- Bde Klengel: Regts. König & Niesemeuchel (2 each), Grenadier Bn Eychelburg

Corps Cavalry (v. Thielmann)
- Bde Gablentz: Regts. Polenz & Prinz Clemens; Saxon Hussars (8)

IX CORPS (Marshal Claude Victor)

12th Division (Partouneaux)
- Bde Billard: 10th & 29th Light (1 each)
- Bde Camus: 44th Line (2); provisional regt. formed from 1 bn each of 36th, 51st & 56th Line
- Bde Blammont: 125th & 126th Line (2 each)

26th Division (Daendels)
- Bde Damas: 1st, 2nd & 4th Berg Regts. (2 each); 3rd Berg Regt. (1)
- Bde Hochberg: 1st-3rd Baden Regts. (2 each), Baden Light Bn
- Bde Prinz Emil of Hesse: Hesse-Darmstadt Leibgarde & Leib-Regt., 8th Westphalian Regt. (2 each); Hesse-Darmstadt Guard Fusiliers (2) joined during the campaign

28th Division (Girard)
- Bde: 4th, 7th & 9th Polish Regts. (2 each; 3rd Bns joined in late September)
- Bde Klengel: Saxon Regts. v. Low & v. Rechten (2 each)

Corps Cavalry (Fournier-Sarlovèze)
- Bde Delatre: Berg Lancers, Hesse-Darmstadt Chevauxlegers
- Bde Fournier: Saxon Regt. Prinz Johann, Baden Hussars

X CORPS (Marshal Jacques-Etienne Macdonald)

7th Division (Grandjean)
- Bde Ricard: 5th Polish Line
- Bde Radziwill: 10th & 11th Polish Line
- Bde Bachelu: 13th Bavarian & 1st Westphalian Line (2 each)

27th (Prussian) Division (Yorck)
- Bde Bulow: 1st & 2nd Combined Regts. (3 each), Fusilier Bn 3rd Regt.
- Bde Horn: 3rd Combined Regt., 9th (Leib) Regt. (3 each)
- Bde Raumer: 5th & 6th Combined Regts. (3 each), East Prussian Jäger Bn

Corps Cavalry
- Bde Huenerbein: Prussian 1st & 2nd Combined Dragoons
- Bde Jeanneret: Prussian 1st & 3rd Combined Hussars

XI CORPS (Marshal Pierre-François Augereau)

30th Division (Heudelet): 1st (3), 6th, 7th (3), 8th, 9th & 17th Provisional Regts.

31st Division (Lagrange): 10th, 11th (3), 12th & 13th (3) Provisional Regts.

32nd Division (Durutte): Regts. Belle Isle, Rhé & Walcheren (French penal corps),

7th Rheinbund Regt. (Würzburg), 1st & 2nd Mediterranean Regts. (all 3 each); Würzburg Chevauxlegers (1 sq)

33rd (Neapolitan) Division (Destrees): Marines, Velites; 5th-7th Line (3 each); Cavalry: Guards of Honour, Velites (2 each)

34th Division (Morand; from October, Loison): 22nd Light (2), 3rd & 105th Line (1 each), 29th & l13th Line (2 each), Saxon Regt. Prinz

Maximilian (2); 4th Westphalian Regt. (2, transferred to IX Corps); Rheinbund Regts.: 3rd (Frankfurt, 3), 4th (Saxon Duchies, 3), 5th (Anhalt & Lippe, 2), 6th (Schwarzburg, Waldeck & Reuss (2)
Corps Cavalry: 4 sq. composed from one coy. each from French 2nd, 5th, 12th, 13th, 14th, 17th, 19th & 20th Dragoons

III CAVALRY CORPS (General Emmanuel Grouchy)
3rd Cuirassier Division (Doumerc)
    Bde Berkheim: 4th Cuirassiers
    Bde l'Heritier: 7th Cuirassiers
    Bde Doullembourg: 14th Cuirassiers, 3rd Chevau-Légers-Lanciers (3)

RUSSIAN ARMY AT BORODINO
(General of Infantry Prince Mikhail Larionovich Kutuzov)

Note: unless stated otherwise in parentheses, infantry regiments had two battalions each, cavalry regiments four squadrons; infantry regiments were brigaded in pairs as stated. Officers of the same name were distinguished by a number after their name according to seniority, e.g. 'Tuchkov I'.

HEADQUARTERS (chief of staff General of Cavalry Count Levin Bennigsen)
2nd Combined Grenadier Bn (from 11th Div), Seleguinsk Regt. (1), Kargopol & Ingermanland Dragoons

FIRST WEST ARMY
(General of Infantry Mikhail Andreas Barclay de Tolly)

II CORPS (Lieutenant General Karl Fedorovich Baggovut)
4th Division (Eugen of Württemberg)
    Tobolsk & Volhynia Regts., Kremenchug & Minsk Regts., 4th & 34th Jägers
17th Division (Alsufev)
    Belozersk & Ryazan Regts., Brest & Wilmanstrand Regts., 30th & 48th Jägers

III CORPS (Lieutenant General Nikolai Tuchkov I)
1st Grenadier Division (Stroganov)
    Lifeguard & Arakcheev Grenadier Regts., Pavlov & Ekaterinoslav Grenadier Regts., St. Petersburg & Tavrichesk Grenadier Regts.
3rd Division (Konovnitsyn)
    Murmansk & Revel Regts., Chernigov & Seleguinsk (1) Regts., 20th & 21st Jägers
Attached
    11th & 41st Jägers, Combined Grenadier Bns of 1st Grenadier & 3rd Divs (1 each), Moscow & Smolensk opolchenie; 6 regts. Cossacks (Karpov)

IV CORPS (Lieutenant General Ivan Ostermann-Tolstoy)
11th Division (Bakhmetiev II)
    Kexholm & Pernau Regts., Elets & Polotsk Regts., 1st & 33rd Jägers
23rd Division (Bakhmetiev I)
    Ekaterinburg & Rylsk Regts., 18th Jägers
Attached
    Kaporsk Regt., Combined Grenadier Bns from 11th & 23rd Divs (1 each)

V CORPS (Grand Duke Constantine)
Lifeguard Division (Lavrov)
    Preobrazhensky & Semonovsky Regts., Ismailovsky & Litovsky Regts., Finland Regt. and Guard Jägers (all these 3 bns each)

Attached
    Combined Grenadier Division: Guard Equipage Bn (1), Combined Grenadiers of 4th & 17th Divs
1st Cuirassier Division (Borozdin II)
    Chevalier Guard, Lifeguard Horse Guards, Emperor's and Empress's Cuirassier Regts.
Attached
    Lifeguard Dragoons

VI CORPS (General of Infantry Dmitri Sergeivich Dokhturov)
7th Division (Kaptsevich)
    Moscow & Pskov Regts., Libau & Sofia Regts., 36th Jägers
24th Division (Likhachev)
    Butyrsk & Shirvan Regts., Tomsk & Ufimsk Regts., 19th & 40th Jägers

I CAVALRY CORPS (General Feodor Petrovich Uvarov)
Lifeguard Cavalry Division
    Lifeguard Hussars, Lancers, Cossacks; Nizhin Dragoons
Attached
    Elisabetgrad Hussars
    Cossacks (General Matvei Ivanovich Platov)

II CAVALRY CORPS (General Friedrich Korff)
6th Bde: Moscow & Pskov Dragoons
8th Bde: Isum Hussars (8), Polish Uhlans (8)
9th Bde: Courland & Orenburg Dragoons
10th Bde: Irkhutsk & Siberian Dragoons
11th Bde: Sumy (8) & Mariupol Hussars

III CAVALRY CORPS (General Peter Pahlen, who was absent; commanded by Kreutz)
1st Bde: Alexandria Hussars (8), Siberian Uhlans
2nd Bde: Smolensk Dragoons

SECOND WEST ARMY
(General of Infantry Peter Bagration)

VII Corps (Lieutenant General Nikolai Raevski)
12th Division (Vasil'chikov)
    Narva & Smolensk Regts., Alexopol & New Ingermanland Regts., 6th Jägers (41st Jägers detached to III Corps)
26th Division (Paskevich)
    Lagoda & Poltava Regts., Nizhegorod & Orel Regts., 5th & 42nd Jägers

VIII CORPS (Lieutenant General Borozdin II)
2nd Grenadier Division (Mecklenburg)
    Kiev & Moscow Grenadiers, Astrakhan & Fanagoria Grenadiers, Little Russia & Siberia Grenadiers
27th Division (Neverovski)
    Odessa & Tarnopol Regts., Simbirsk & Vilensk Regts., 49th & 50th Jägers
2nd Combined Grenadier Division (Vorontsov)
    Combined grenadiers of 2nd, 12th & 26th Divs (2 each)

IV CAVALRY CORPS (Major General Count Sievers)
4th Cavalry Division (Sievers)
    12th Bde: Chernigov & Kharkov Dragoons (serving dismounted)
    13th Bde: Kiev & New Russia Dragoons
    14th Bde: Akhtyrka Hussars (8), Lithuanian Uhlans (8)
2nd Cuirassier Division (Duka)
    2nd Bde: Ekaterinoslav & Military Order Cuirassiers
    3rd Bde: Gluchov, Little Russia & Novgorod Cuirassiers

THE INVASION

Having failed to bring the Tsar to heel by diplomatic means and threats, Napoleon had to decide the route he should take in pursuit of destroying the Russian field army. There were two possible fronts, separated by the Pripet marshes that extended roughly from Brest-Litovsk on the river Bug south-west to the area north and west of Kiev, a swampy region with few roads and thus unsuitable for large-scale military operations. To the north of this morass, stretching virtually to the Baltic, was a somewhat barren region running from the Duchy of Warsaw to Smolensk, becoming more fertile as the route ran eastwards towards Moscow. River lines ran across this path, but none were insurmountable; the most westerly, the Niemen, had major crossing points at Kovno in the north of the sector and Grodno in the south. South of the Pripet marshes the area was more fertile, notably around Kiev, but the river lines were more defensible, and an advance from that region towards Smolensk would have stretched an army's line of communications. Furthermore, south of the Pripet marshes was a population irrevocably hostile, whereas west of the Niemen at least the Polish inhabitants would be supportive. It was thus on the northern front that Napoleon determined to make his advance.

He planned to cross the line of the Niemen on its northerly section, in the vicinity of Kovno, advance eastwards on Vilna and towards Vitebsk, from which position he could threaten either Moscow, further east, or the capital, St Petersburg, to the north. His desire, however, was to smash the Russian army before such considerations became necessary. Napoleon was aware of the Russian dispositions and the nature of their commanders, and calculated accordingly. On the south of his line of operations Schwarzenberg and Jérôme would occupy the Russian forces in their front while Napoleon's main army crossed the Niemen to engage Barclay's First West Army. Bagration might be tempted to move westwards along the line of the river Bug and towards the Vistula, but if he were to fall back, Jérôme could advance and engage him. Eugène's army was to hold the right flank of Napoleon's own advance, to maintain contact with Jérôme and engage Bagration should he advance north, while on the extreme left of Napoleon's front Macdonald would advance on Riga, outflanking Barclay's right. Then as Barclay fell back as anticipated, or moved southwards towards Bagration, Napoleon planned to swing his army right, enveloping the Russian flank and rear, trapping them against the Bug or Vistula in the west and with the marshes at their back. From this position they would be compelled to fight, outnumbered by the concentration of Napoleon's forces, or, as at Ulm in the classic manoeuvre of 1805, be forced to capitulate. Napoleon was confident that these manoeuvres would bring

The line of Napoleon's advance to Borodino

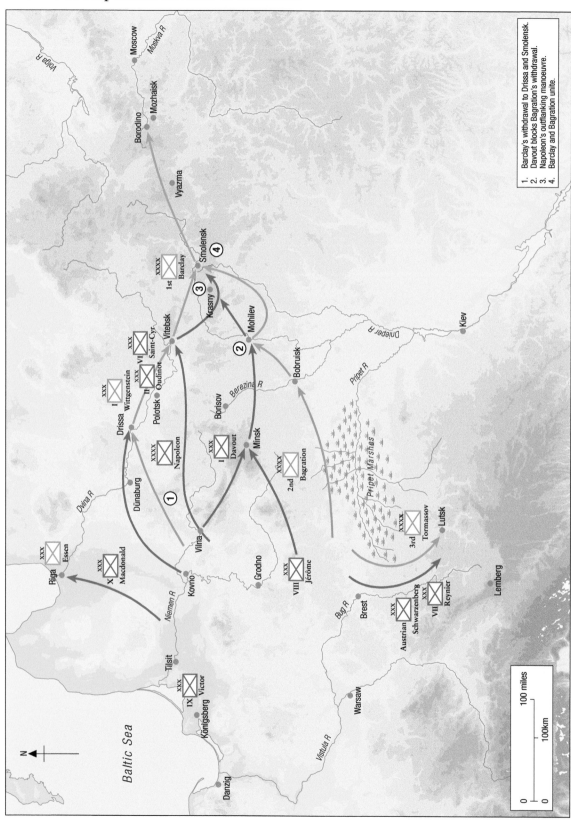

1. Barclay's withdrawal to Drissa and Smolensk.
2. Davout blocks Bagration's withdrawal.
3. Napoleon's outflanking manoeuvre.
4. Barclay and Bagration unite.

about the great battle he desired, and thus decide the campaign in a few weeks; but the planning was complicated by the question of scale, the distances involved being enormous, making the coordination of movements fraught with hazard.

The Tsar's strategy had much less potential, and was complicated by divisions within the Russian command. As Minister of War Barclay nominally had authority over Bagration's army, but he and other generals were senior to him, and the Tsar was greatly influenced by his Prussian advisor, Colonel Ernst von Phull, a pedantic crank with flawed theories. Clausewitz, who worked with him, described him as:

> a man of much understanding and cultivation, but without a knowledge of actual things; he had... led a life so secluded and contemplative that he knew nothing of the occurrences of the daily world... he had framed for himself a one-sided and meagre system of war, which could stand the test neither of philosophical investigation, nor historical comparison... The author never saw a man who lost his head so easily, who, intent as he ever was on great things, was so soon overwhelmed by the least of little realities.
>
> Clausewitz, C. M. von, *The Campaign of 1812 in Russia*, London, 1843, pp. 5–9.

Phull conceived a plan in which one of the Russian armies should retire, drawing Napoleon forwards, while the other cut his communications or assailed his flank. He thought that if Barclay were attacked he should fall back to an entrenched camp being constructed at Drissa, on the river Dvina, mid-way and slightly to the north of a line between Kovno and Smolensk, the camp perhaps inspired by Frederick the Great's famous entrenched position at Bunzelwitz in 1761. It was intended that as Napoleon advanced on this feature, Bagration should move up from the south and attack his right flank; though Barclay's retirement to this position would actually widen the gap between the two Russian armies that could be exploited by Napoleon.

The Grande Armée crosses the Niemen. (Print after F. de Myrbach)

LEFT

Napoleon reconnoitring, wearing his habitual campaign uniform of a grey greatcoat over the undress uniform of the Chasseurs à Cheval of the Imperial Guard. (Print after Raffet)

RIGHT

The advance of the Grande Armée was shadowed and watched by Russian light troops, notably Cossacks, whose most effective role was in reconnoitring and harassing the enemy.

When Napoleon arrived at the army's headquarters in mid-June 1812 his troops were moving into position, and on 22 June, in disguise, he made a personal reconnaissance of the Niemen and selected crossing points. On the following day three pontoon bridges were in position and the campaign began by the leading elements of the Grande Armée crossing the Niemen.

From the beginning, Napoleon's advance did not go entirely to plan. Barclay was not encountered, for when he learned of the invasion he commenced a withdrawal upon Drissa and the line of the Dvina, while Bagration also began to pull back, with the intention of uniting with Barclay. Napoleon found that he could not advance as swiftly as he had intended; initially the weather was hot and dry, but heavy rain from 29 June turned the roads to mud, slowing especially the artillery and supply trains. Murat's cavalry was racing ahead towards Vilna, threatening to outdistance support, while Napoleon was more concerned about securing his left flank, against which the Russian I Corps of General Ludwig Wittgenstein (a second-generation German in Russian service) posed a threat; part of Barclay's army, it was retiring rather more slowly. Napoleon had Oudinot's corps on his left, with Macdonald much further left, to guard against a counterattack in that sector; but on the right of the main advance, Napoleon had to delay until Eugène's army should come up, behind schedule on account of the transportation problems. Until then he dare not move too far lest his line of communication be cut by Bagration.

Napoleon occupied Vilna without a fight on 28 June, and as Barclay had not stood to fight, he switched his attention to Bagration to the south, who was also withdrawing. Leaving Murat to follow Barclay, with Oudinot and Ney in support, Napoleon devised a trap: Davout was ordered south-eastwards towards Minsk, to cut off Bagration's most direct route to Barclay, while Jérôme was to march east and trap Bagration between himself and Davout. The plan failed completely; intelligence was poor and Jérôme so dilatory that Bagration evaded the trap and continued his withdrawal by a more southerly route. Napoleon berated Jérôme for his slowness, and Davout, still attempting to engage Bagration, marched further south-east, towards Mohilev, and informed Jérôme that he was taking command of the entire right wing. This proved the final insult for Jérôme; he resigned his command and returned home to Westphalia.

After Bagration's escape, Napoleon switched his attention back to Barclay, whose army reached Drissa on 10–11 July, to find the position badly sited and incapable of fulfilling its intended role. At this point the Tsar, who had been with the First West Army, was persuaded that his time would be spent more valuably mobilizing reinforcements, so he left the field headquarters on 19 July, his departure permitting Barclay to exercise command with rather more freedom.

Having no desire to attack entrenched positions, Napoleon planned another outflanking manoeuvre. Leaving Murat, with Oudinot and Ney, to hold the front of the Drissa position, he intended to swing around Barclay's left and threaten his communications with St Petersburg. Leaving Wittgenstein to block the road to St Petersburg, Barclay abandoned the Drissa position and began to march south-east, upon Vitebsk, hoping to be joined there by Bagration. Davout, however, still endeavouring to prevent such a union, blocked Bagration's path in a sharp action at Mohilev on 23 July. Napoleon followed Barclay, and Murat's cavalry engaged Russian forces at Ostrovno, west of Vitebsk, on 25–26 July; but Napoleon delayed for more support to arrive. He missed his opportunity for Barclay, realizing that Bagration could not join him at Vitebsk, recommenced his south-eastwards withdrawal, making the ancient city of Smolensk the new point of rendezvous. Again Napoleon had failed to trap his enemy.

Despite not having been engaged in a minor battle, even at this early stage of the campaign Napoleon's army was suffering considerable losses. The hot weather had compounded sickness within the army, considerable numbers of horses had been lost and there were great difficulties maintaining the supply system, requiring troops to forage. Napoleon was compelled to halt at Vitebsk to regroup and allow supplies to arrive.

Although Napoleon had not been able to engage the enemy as he had intended, there was greater activity to the north, where Oudinot engaged in a protracted struggle against Wittgenstein in the vicinity of Polotsk. A major battle was fought on 18 August; on 16 August Oudinot had been reinforced

LEFT
One of the Russian scouts (centre) was captured and interrogated in person by Eugène de Beauharnais (right) but subsequently escaped custody. The guard (left) is Eugène's loyal Mameluke servant, who disappeared during the retreat. (Print after Albrecht Adam)

RIGHT
On the march: Eugène de Beauharnais in an improvised bivouac on the night of 8–9 July. Eugène (left) lies on a heap of straw while his aide, Général de Brigade Joseph Triaire, has a simple bed. The sentry is a member of the Italian Guards of Honour. (Print after Albrecht Adam)

The weariness of the march into Russia is exemplified by this scene recorded by Albrecht Adam, showing Italians of Pino's Division of IV Corps; an exhausted soldier trudges onwards supported by a comrade who carries both their muskets, while a mounted officer carries both men's knapsacks.

by Gouvion Saint-Cyr's VI Corps, and it was Saint-Cyr who took over after Oudinot was wounded, winning a victory that both removed the pressure on Napoleon's left flank and secured him his marshal's baton. In the south, the advance of Tormasov's Third West Army to the vicinity of Brest-Litovsk was held in check by Reynier's VII Corps, but Schwarzenberg had to be ordered up in support.

Frustrating Napoleon's plans, the First and Second West Armies united in the vicinity of Smolensk in early August, and, stung by criticism of his continuing retreat, Barclay decided to take the offensive. Following a council of war, on 6 August he marched westwards from Smolensk, intending to catch Napoleon while his army was resting. Napoleon's reconnaissance facility was always impaired by the presence of Cossacks who hovered around the flanks of the Grande Armée, but they were usually more of an irritation than a serious threat. Yet on 8 August Platov surprised and mauled General Sebastiani's 2nd Light Cavalry Division near Inkovo. It was not the only time Sebastiani was caught off-guard during the campaign, leading to his nickname 'General Surprise', but it was still unusual for Cossacks to defeat regular cavalry in such a manner. Instead of it acting to spur Barclay's offensive intentions, his nerve seems to have failed to a degree and he began to move north-west instead of mounting a serious offensive.

Realizing that Barclay was not pressing ahead, Napoleon resumed the plan formulated before Inkovo, an outflanking manoeuvre to turn the Russian left, cut the road linking Smolensk and Moscow and force Barclay to fight. On the night of 13–14 August pontoon bridges were thrown over the Dnieper, and by the morning of the 14th some 175,000 men were across and marching east, preparing to swing southwards of Smolensk. Speed was essential to reach Napoleon's desired position and by mid-afternoon they had reached Krasny, south-west of Smolensk, and it is possible that the cavalry advance-guard could have reached that city by nightfall; but the plan was thwarted. To guard the approach to Smolensk, Barclay had posted General Dmitri Neverovski with his 27th Division and some cavalry, totalling about 9,500 men, near Krasny. Murat attempted to sweep them aside but mishandled the action, making repeated cavalry attacks instead of awaiting the arrival of Ney's III Corps. Forming his infantry – many inexperienced – into hollow squares,

Neverovski conducted a skilful withdrawal along the Smolensk road, until Murat called off his attacks towards nightfall; as Wilson remarked, Neverovski's small command had lost 1,500 men and five guns, 'but acquired for its commander and itself much honour'[8]; and, more importantly, had frustrated Napoleon's manoeuvre.

Neverovski reported Napoleon's advance to Bagration, whose army had remained in the vicinity of Smolensk rather than following Barclay, and he sent General Nikolai Raevski's VII Corps in support. He reinforced the Smolensk garrison and moved down the Krasny road, meeting Neverovski and pulling back towards the city. When he learned of Napoleon's manoeuvre, Barclay abandoned his forward movement and turned to return to Smolensk.

SMOLENSK

Despite the need for speed, Napoleon halted on 15 August to consolidate (and, being his birthday, to hold a somewhat unnecessary review), so that not until the following day did he close on Smolensk. The old city was protected by a massive wall strengthened by towers, but it was encircled by suburbs that could provide cover for an attacker. Raevski advanced his defensive line into these suburbs on the south bank of the Dnieper, south and west of the city.

The first of Napoleon's forces to arrive, on the morning of 16 August, were Ney's III Corps and Murat's cavalry, but despite some action in the afternoon they were not sufficiently strong to make a serious attempt on the defences. Later in the day Davout's I Corps and Poniatowski's V Corps arrived to complete the encirclement of the southern part of the city, Ney on the left, Poniatowski on the right. Raevski rejoined Bagration's army north-east of the city, its defence being entrusted to General Dmitri Dokhturov. Early on 17 August he cleared the French outposts from the suburbs, but in the afternoon Napoleon ordered an assault from three sides, and despite supporting fire from Russian artillery on the far bank of the Dnieper, the defenders were forced back within the city walls. Napoleon mounted a bombardment by some 150 guns and gained a foothold within the defences, but he was beaten back by a counterattack by Prince Eugen of Württemberg, whose division from II Corps had been sent by Barclay to bolster the defences. Another assault was made at about seven in the evening, but the Russians held firm.

Napoleon's assault had cost him about 10,000 casualties for little progress. It might have been more effective to bypass the city, march eastwards and attempt to cut the road from Smolensk to Moscow, but perhaps Napoleon thought that the storm of so important a city would convince the Tsar to negotiate; though if it had any effect it served only to stiffen the Russian will to resist. The threat to communications, however, probably influenced Barclay's decision to continue his withdrawal, despite the outrage and accusations of cowardice that it provoked, and Dokhturov evacuated the city on the night of 17–18 August. On the morning of the 18th Ney made an attempt to cross the river in pursuit but was blocked by Bagration's rearguard. Bagration began to retire before Barclay, opening a gap between their armies, but Napoleon failed to exploit it, a lack of urgency compounded by imperfect intelligence of the Russian situation. When it became obvious that they were heading for Moscow, Napoleon began his pursuit in earnest on 19 August,

The battle for Smolensk

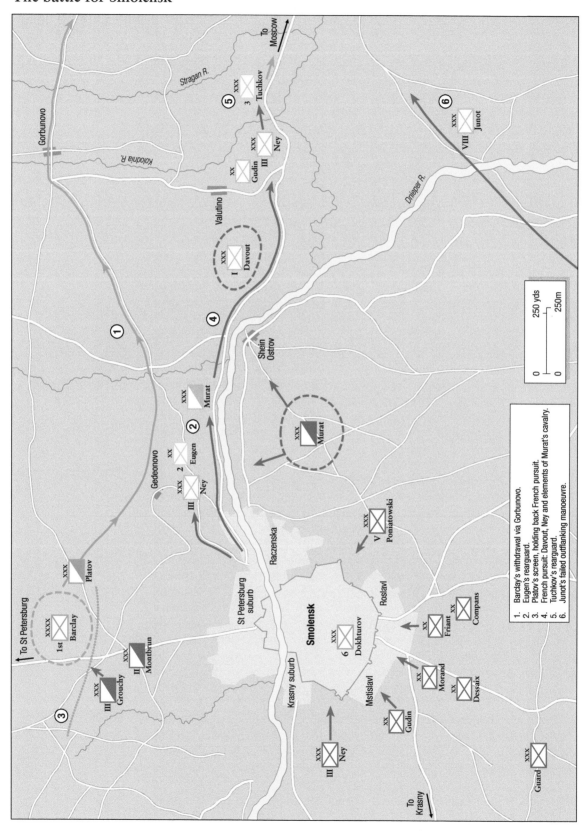

1. Barclay's withdrawal via Gorbunovo.
2. Eugen's rearguard.
3. Platov's screen, holding back French pursuit.
4. French pursuit: Davout, Ney and elements of Murat's cavalry.
5. Tuchkov's rearguard.
6. Junot's failed outflanking manoeuvre.

Murat and Ney, with Davout following, pressing against Bagration's rearguard, consisting primarily of General Nikolai Tuchkov's III Corps and Eugen of Württemberg's division.

Napoleon assigned a crucial task to the newly arrived VIII Corps, Jérôme's old command, now led by General Jean-Andoche Junot. He was ordered to cross the Dnieper and rush around the Russian left flank to block their line of retreat; but Junot was not the ideal commander for this duty. As Napoleon's vanguard battled the Russian rearguard at Valutino, and further east towards Lubino, Junot struggled to get his command over the Dnieper, and then declined to attack the Russian left despite the entreaties of his subordinates and even Murat. Ney and elements of Davout's corps pressed back Tuchkov's rearguard, but were unable to make the necessary progress, and in the action lost a most valuable and experienced divisional commander long associated with Davout, General Charles-Etienne Gudin de la Sablonnière, mortally wounded by a roundshot that broke both legs. With the outflanking manoeuvre having failed, Barclay was able to withdraw successfully. Napoleon put the blame squarely upon Junot, who he later remarked 'gave me great cause of dissatisfaction; he was no longer the same man, and committed some gross blunders which cost us dear'[9]; yet Napoleon could have been there in person to coordinate manoeuvres, had he not retired to Smolensk earlier in the day. (Less than a year later Junot's mental health broke down completely and he died after leaping from a window.)

Having once more failed to force the Russians to fight a decisive engagement, Napoleon had reached a critical point in the campaign. He had articulated a prudent course of action before the Russians had left Smolensk, in a discussion with Armand de Caulaincourt, ex-ambassador to Russia, who

Near Ostrovno, 25 July: elements of I Cavalry Corps with Eugène de Beauharnais. The troops in the foreground are from Bruyères's 1st Light Cavalry Division. (Print after Albrecht Adam)

was present with Napoleon's headquarters: 'by abandoning Smolensk, which is one of their Holy Cities, the Russian generals are dishonouring their arms in the eyes of their own people. That will put me in a strong position.... I will dig myself in... my army will be more formidable and my position more menacing to the Russians than as if I had won two battles'[10], and he would still be able to threaten either Moscow or St Petersburg. Conversely, a long stay in the region would put additional strain upon the system of logistics, especially as the rains of autumn and winter would cause the roads to deteriorate; it would allow the Tsar to regroup and gather strength, and hesitation could have political repercussions given the lukewarm support of Prussia and Austria. The alternative was to continue the pursuit of the Russian army towards Moscow, which Napoleon was convinced the Tsar would have to fight to defend, though this would over-extend Napoleon's line of communications and make his flanks more vulnerable. A march on Moscow, some 450km (280 miles) east of Smolensk, would also continue to weaken the Grande Armée that was already suffering severely. The loss of horses was becoming critical, a point made forcibly to Napoleon by Murat's chief of staff, General Auguste Belliard; but Caulaincourt recalled that Napoleon took no notice, apparently considering that any price was worth paying to engage the enemy.

Napoleon decided that there was a more convincing case for continuing the pursuit and ending the campaign with a victory, than in delaying a resumption of hostilities until the spring of 1813. The cautious Caulaincourt stated that wisdom had been overtaken by the enticement of glory, though Napoleon stated that within a month they would be in Moscow and have peace in six weeks. On 25 August the Grande Armée renewed its eastward march.

KUTUZOV TAKES COMMAND

Within the Russian command there was internal turmoil: many had lost all confidence in Barclay, unpopular in some quarters as a 'foreigner' even before his perceived unwillingness to stand and fight. The Tsar had determined on absolute inflexibility; no compromise while invaders were still on Russian soil, and his appeals united Russian society into a mood of resistance combining patriotism with religious fervour: for example, the famous icon of the Black Virgin of Smolensk, regarded as a sacred talisman, was entrusted to the care of the army, and it was stated that peasants rushed to join the fighting shouting 'Tis the will of God!'[11] The crisis within the Russian command was witnessed by Sir Robert Wilson:

> A change of chief had become indispensable. Barclay no longer could command any confidence in his judgement or firmness of purpose. He had seemed to be governed by a chapter of accidents, and to have wasted his force by continual movements without explicable or defined object. The spirit of the army was affected by a sense of mortification, and all ranks loudly and boldly complained, discontent was general, and discipline relaxing... the difficulties of Barclay... were immensely beyond his capacity to regulate satisfactorily or to overcome... he was a brave soldier and a good officer, but not a captain with a master mind equal to the need.
> Wilson, Sir Robert, *Narrative of Events during the Invasion of Russia by Napoleon Bonaparte*, ed. Revd. H. Randolph, London, 1860, p. 130

The solution arrived at by the Tsar and his advisors was to install a new commander over both Barclay and Bagration: Mikhail Kutuzov. Sixty-seven years of age, he was one of the outstanding Russian soldiers of his time; a disciple of the great Suvarov, he had seen much active service and in campaigning against the Turks had been shot in the head with the loss of an eye. Commanding the Russian forces in the 1805 campaign, he had attempted to prevent the Austro-Russian army from fighting at Austerlitz, so his reputation had not suffered from that defeat. He was not, however, popular with the Tsar and since then had been employed largely in administrative duties until returning to field command against the Turks in 1811.

Wilson described Kutuzov as:

> A bon vivant – polished, courteous, shrewd as a Greek, naturally intelligent as an Asiatic and well instructed as a European – he was more disposed to trust to diplomacy for his success than to martial prowess, for which by his age and the state of his constitution he was no longer qualified. When he joined the army he was… though hale, so very corpulent and unwieldy that he was obliged to move about, even when in the field, in a little four-wheeled carriage.
> Wilson, *Narrative*, p. 131

Clausewitz also knew him personally and recalled that he was 'no longer in possession of the activity of mind and body… In these respects he was inferior to Barclay, but in natural qualities certainly superior. Kutuzov had been in youth what the French call a sabreur [swashbuckler], and united with this much cleverness, cunning, and dexterity.'[12] The Tsar told Wilson that Kutuzov was the general who 'the nobility of Russia had selected to vindicate the arms of Russia'[13], and despite the Tsar's reservations his appointment was greeted by widespread joy: 'there was in his person… the stamp of an ancient Muscovite, an air of nationality, which rendered him dear to the Russians: at Moscow the joy at his appointment had been carried to intoxication; people embraced one another in the streets, and considered themselves as saved'[14].

Artillery of the Grande Armée moves up to the firing line, at Ostrovno, 26 July. (Print after Albrecht Adam)

Clausewitz remarked on the reaction of the military: 'Kutuzov's arrival excited new confidence in the army; the evil genius of the foreigners was exorcised by a true Russian, a Suvarov on a small scale, and it was not doubted that a battle would ensue without delay'[15].

Kutuzov was confirmed in his command on 20 August, and set off to join the army without much delay. He selected as chief of staff the Hanoverian Levin Bennigsen, who had served Russia since 1773 and had been implicated in the conspiracy that led to the assassination of Tsar Paul I, father of the current Tsar; he was the commander defeated at Eylau and Friedland and was far from an ideal choice.

Despite losing the chief command, Barclay dutifully served on as leader of First West Army, and continued to supervise the withdrawal of the Russian forces towards Moscow. He passed through Vyazma on 27 August, burning the supplies left there, a 'scorched earth' tactic intended to deny provisions and fodder to the foraging Grande Armée. Barclay's retreat arrived at Tsarevo, mid-way between Smolensk and Moscow, but his intention to stand there was overtaken by the arrival of Kutuzov. Clausewitz likened the continuing withdrawal to the stagger of a man who had lost his balance, and that Kutuzov needed some time to restore the army's equilibrium.

Recognizing that the army was weary and in need of reinforcement, Kutuzov recommenced the withdrawal almost immediately on taking command, while assuring the Tsar that he would fight to defend Moscow. He requested supplies from the governor of Moscow, Feodor Rostopchin, but the only reinforcement he received were some 16,000 mostly new recruits under General Mikhail Miloradovich, and about 15,000 ill-equipped and partially trained *opolchenie*. This brought the total of the combined army to about 120,000 men or slightly more.

Pursuing the Russians, Napoleon still had a formidable force despite his losses. It is difficult to be precise about the numbers involved at any one point in the campaign; for example, the number of stragglers or those who temporarily fell ill is unknown. (To remedy this problem, on 2 September Napoleon issued an order to collect all men who were lingering behind their units, to maximize strength as battle was imminent.) Estimates of Napoleon's strength at this period range from 156,000 to as low as 115,000 present in the forthcoming battle. His army comprised the Imperial Guard, Murat's four cavalry corps, Davout's I Corps, Ney's III Corps, Eugène's IV Corps, two of the three divisions of Poniatowski's V Corps (Dombrowski's division had been detached earlier and was not present), and Junot's VIII Corps. Wilson, who estimated Napoleon's strength at 140,000, stated that, 'The infantry was reported in good order, but the cavalry was generally in bad condition from fatigue, and from want of good water and proper food. Murat one day complaining to Nansouty that "the cavalry had not vigorously executed a charge", Nansouty is said to have replied, "The horses have no patriotism: the soldiers fight without bread, but the horses insist on oats".'[16] Napoleon's army marched in three principal columns, the main body in the centre with Eugène on the left and Poniatowski on the right.

As his withdrawal continued, Kutuzov reached Gzhatsk on the night of 30–31 August, where he considered making his stand; but Bennigsen claimed to have found a better position, about 40km (25 miles) further east, near the village of Borodino. Its defensive qualities were confirmed by Barclay's staff officer, the Livonian Colonel Carl Friedrich von Toll, and Kutuzov accepted that it was there he should give battle. It was some 115km (70 miles) west of Moscow.

8. Wilson, *Narrative*, p. 83.
9. Las Cases, Vol. II p. 394.
10. Caulaincourt, A. de, *With Napoleon in Russia: The Memoirs of General de Caulaincourt, Duke of Vicenza*, New York, 1935, p. 75.
11. Ségur, Vol. I p. 307.
12. Clausewitz, C. M. von, *The Campaign of 1812 in Russia*, London, 1843, pp. 139–40.
13. Wilson, *Narrative*, p. 131.
14. Ségur, Vol. I pp. 307–08.
15. Clausewitz, p. 139.
16. Wilson, *Narrative*. p. 133.

THE BATTLE OF BORODINO

THE BATTLEFIELD

The field chosen by the Russians was not dominated by any precipitous feature that could be defended easily, but its strategic position was significant: what was to become the Russian front line ran across both the highways from Smolensk to Moscow, the Old and New Smolensk roads, to south and north respectively, which converged east of the battlefield at Mozhaisk. To the north-east of this front line ran the Moskva River, which played no part in the battle beyond providing the name for what Napoleon called the battle – 'Moscowa' in the common French spelling – perhaps to emphasize that he was fighting for possession of Moscow. Much more significant was the Kolotcha stream that ran in a roughly south-west to north-east direction across the Russian front, although the only protection it provided was to Kutuzov's right-centre and right flank. The village of Borodino was on the west bank of the Kolotcha, separated by it from the main Russian position, reducing its tactical value; it was bridged there, but as Wilson remarked, the Kolotcha was fordable everywhere although running in parts through a 'deep ravine'. Joining the Kolotcha just south-west of Borodino was the Semenovka stream, which ran in front of the Russian centre; and adjoining that, before the Russian left, was the Kamenka stream. Together they produced a waterway that ran in front almost the whole of the Russian position, of varying tactical significance, though even the lesser banks would prove something of an obstacle for an attacker.

Wilson described the whole position as 'broken, billowy, and uneven', and noted that the left especially – that not protected by the Kolotcha – though open was intersected with ravines and brushwood, which 'rendered approach difficult for compact bodies'[17]. To the rear of the Russian left-centre was the small village of Semenovskaya; being largely wooden-built it was partly dismantled by the Russian army before the battle. The higher ground, though not so steep as to present an insurmountable object to an attacker, included a raise around the hamlet of Gorki on the right-centre, where Kutuzov was to establish his headquarters, and two prominences in the centre on either side of the Semenovka stream. At the extreme left of the Russian front was the hamlet of Utitsa, on the Old Smolensk Road, to the south of which was a prehistoric prominence that later became known as the 'Utitsa mound'. On the left especially there were copses of birch and pine, some of this brushwood sheltering the Russian front line. Clausewitz commented that the terrain on the left comprised only 'some hillocks with a gentle slope, and perhaps twenty feet high, together with strips of scrubby wood, formed so confused a whole, that it was difficult to pronounce which party would have the advantage of the ground'[18].

Exemplifying his determination to stand and fight, Kutuzov ordered the construction of fieldworks to bolster his position. In addition to positions for artillery batteries like that established just west of Gorki, and the village of Borodino being put into a state of defence, three principal fortifications were constructed as strongly as permitted by the limited time available. The best known of these was that established on the rising ground between Gorki and Semenovskaya, which became known as the 'Great Redoubt' or 'Raevski Redoubt'. It was about 180m (590ft) long, consisting of an earthwork rampart with a short *epaulements* (breastworks to protect against enfilade fire) at each flank; 12-pdr artillery pieces were placed in the work, apparently 19 in number (though the number is sometimes stated to be 18 to 21). The raising of the earthwork created a ditch in front, and some *trous de loup* or 'wolf pits' were dug beyond that to hinder the approach of the enemy, but the limited time available and the stony nature of the ground limited the strength of the construction. Despite some palisading its rear was largely open.

The second of the principal Russian defences was a group of three smaller earthworks that came to be known as the 'Bagration *flèches*' ('flèches' from being arrow-shaped), to the south of the Semenovka stream, to the left-centre of Kutuzov's position; Wilson thought that their purpose was to support the Russian skirmishers who would be thrown forward of the main position. About 1.5km (1 mile) west of the *flèches* was the third major earthwork, known as the 'Shevardino Redoubt' from the name of the nearby hamlet. It was constructed at Toll's suggestion as an observation post from which to discern the approach of Napoleon's army and to delay any rapid attack against the Semenovskaya area, but it was so far advanced from the main position that it would be impossible to hold.

Kutuzov drew up his line in preparation for the arrival of Napoleon's army. Its front was long, about 7.3km (4½ miles), running from the banks of the Moskva in the north to Utitsa and the Old Smolensk Road in the south, although as Wilson pointed out, the principal battle-front was considerably shorter, about 4.5km (3 miles), running from Borodino village to Utitsa. The right half of the line was assigned to Barclay's First West Army; Bagration's Second West Army held the left of the line. Excluding the skirmish-screen of Cossacks on the extreme flank, the right of the line was occupied by II Corps of General Karl Baggovut, with IV Corps of General Alexander Ivanovich Ostermann-Tolstoy to his left. Both these formations were protected by the Kolotcha stream running in their front, and in their rear was Platov with the main body of his Cossacks and I Cavalry Corps of General Feodor Uvarov in support. The right-centre, running from Ostermann-Tolstoy's position to the Great Redoubt, was held by General Dmitri Dokhturov's VI Corps, and in reserve were II and III Cavalry Corps led by Generals Korff and Kreutz respectively, the latter in temporary command due to the absence of General Peter Pahlen, nominal commander of the corps.

From this point the line southwards was held by Bagration's Second West Army. Raevski's VII Corps was detailed to hold the region of the Redoubt that was to bear his name, and the line as far as Semenovskaya; in support was General Count Sievers' IV Cavalry Corps. South of Semenovskaya, covering the *flèches*, was General Borozdin's VIII Corps, of which General

Borodino, the opening dispositions

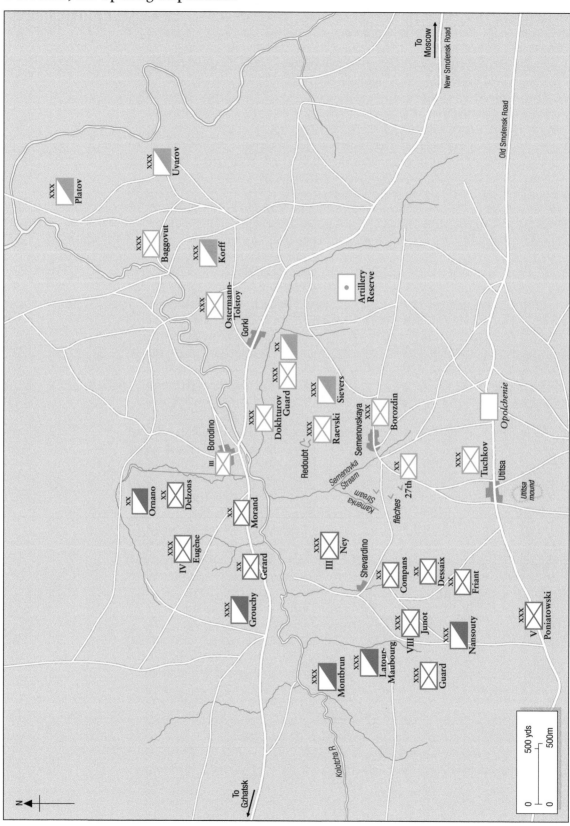

Vorontsov's 2nd Grenadier Division was in the *flèches*, with General Neverovski's brave 27th Division in support. As a general reserve, for deployment on either flank as required, was Grand Duke Constantine's V Corps (the Imperial Lifeguard), the 1st and 2nd Cuirassier Divisions, General Nikolai Tuchkov's III Corps and the artillery reserve. Most of the *opolchenie* units were held to the rear of the main line.

The strongest part of Kutuzov's line was his right, his concentration on that flank suggesting that he expected Napoleon's main drive to be along the New Smolensk Road, while the left, despite the bolstering of earthworks, was weak; Clausewitz commented that, 'The best side of the position… the right wing, could be of no avail to redeem the defects of the left', and that the extreme strength of the right represented 'a useless squandering of troops'. He also thought that the Russian disposition was too narrow from front to rear, that the reserves were too close to the firing-line, and attributed this, after discussions with that officer, to Toll's influence. The cavalry, he stated, was posted only 300 to 400 paces behind the front line, and the main reserve scarcely 1,000 paces further back, so that they suffered from enemy fire even while in reserve. Clausewitz believed that had they been posted further back they could have been concealed more easily and have been used with greater freedom to move to the flanks. He also observed that the Russian artillery took up more space than that of any other army due to the number of small ammunition carts that it used, so that with the number of guns involved, and the proximity of reserves, the area behind the firing-line was 'filled and crammed up'.

The Russian command structure included an additional tier between corps and army commanders: on the right, General Mikhail Miloradovich had jurisdiction over the corps of Baggovut and Ostermann-Tolstoy, and the cavalry of Uvarov and Korff; Raevski's and Borozdin's corps, and Sievers's cavalry, came under the authority of Prince Andrei Gorchakov; Dokhturov had authority over his own corps and Kreutz's cavalry, and Grand Duke Constantine led the whole reserve.

There are various estimates of the strength of the Russian army at the commencement of the battle, but the approximate strength seems to have been about 72,000 infantry, 17,500 cavalry, and 7,000 Cossacks; about 14,300 artillery (including five engineer companies) in 55 batteries with a total of 640 pieces of artillery; and 10,000 *opolchenie*. (Sir Robert Wilson's estimate of 'effective regulars' was 90,000, which may include a deduction for troops detached to rear areas.)

NAPOLEON'S ARRIVAL AND THE SHEVARDINO REDOUBT

On 5 September the Grande Armée began to arrive to the west of the Russian position, initially Murat's advance-guard of cavalry supported by General Jean-Dominique Compans's division of I Corps. They found Russian skirmishers thrown out the west of the Shevardino Redoubt, as far as the west bank of the Kolotcha, but they were pushed back in the direction of the Redoubt. In the afternoon Napoleon rode forward in person to survey the position, and finding that the Redoubt would greatly inhibit the deployment of his right wing, determined to capture it.

Defence of the Shevardino Redoubt had been entrusted by Gorchakov to Neverovski's 27th Division, which was deployed in columns behind it; the

Skirmishers were thrown out from the main Russian positions at Borodino and were the first to engage the Grande Armée as it advanced. This French skirmisher is replenishing his supply of cartridges from the pouch of a fallen comrade, as Russians (right) continue to fire.

Redoubt itself held 12 guns, with Neverovski's two Jäger regiments (49th and 50th), reinforced by the 5th Jägers from the 26th Division, with a considerable force of cavalry including the 2nd Cuirassier Division and four dragoon regiments from IV Cavalry Corps. To assault the position Napoleon deployed three divisions of Davout's I Corps: Compans's Division to attack the redoubt itself, and those of Morand and Friant to move against Shevardino village to the north of the Redoubt, with I and II Cavalry Corps in support. Poniatowski's V Corps was advanced to a position south of the Redoubt. Compans's artillery bombarded the Redoubt and despite charges by Russian cavalry, after a severe contest the French 57th and 61st Line stormed into the position. The fighting was confused but Wilson stated that the Russians retook the position at least twice, Bagration bringing up the 2nd Grenadier Division of Prince Karl von Mecklenburg from VIII Corps, which stormed in again; Russian cavalry charges included that by the Little Russia and Gluchov Cuirassiers which overran part of Compans's artillery and brought off some guns. Fighting continued until darkness fell, by which time Poniatowski was turning the Russian left; and Kutuzov ordered Bagration to withdraw to the main Russian position. Both sides had lost heavily, estimates of Napoleon's casualties ranging from 4,000 to 8,000 men and five guns, while a figure of between 6,000 to 8,000 Russians was quoted.

Eugène Labaume, a staff officer with Eugène de Beauharnais, recounted an anecdote that exemplifies the cost of capturing the redoubt: on the following day Napoleon reviewed the 61st Line, 'which had suffered most, [and] asked the colonel what he had done with one of his battalions. Sire, replied he, it is in the redoubt'[19]. (Gaspard Gourgaud, on Napoleon's staff at the time, as part of his vehement attack on Ségur's account of the campaign, claimed that it was four fieldpieces firing grapeshot that had compelled the Russians to abandon the position, and denied the veracity of this story.)

As night drew on, recalled Labaume, 'Scarcely had we ceased firing, when the Russians, encamped as it were on an amphitheatre, lighted innumerable fires. The resplendent brightness, gave the hill an enchanting aspect, and formed a striking contrast with our camp; where the soldiers, deprived of every thing, reposed amidst all the horrors of war, hearing nothing around them but the groans of the wounded.'[20] The Russians were not inactive, however, for an important change in their dispositions was made. Napoleon's activity on the Russian left suggested that he might be intending to advance up the Old Smolensk Road, which compelled Kutuzov to reinforce his left flank. From the reserve he sent Tuchkov's III Corps, with about 1,500 Cossacks and 7,000 *opolchenie*, into the woods around Utitsa, intending them to remain under cover until Napoleon advanced down the road, when an ambush could be sprung against his flank and rear. Linking Tuchkov's command with Bagration's left, a skirmish-line of Jägers was strung out between the two. On the eve of the battle Bennigsen visited this section of the army and found the commanders of the Jägers nervous of their exposed position; so to support them he ordered Tuchkov to abandon the ambush and move his troops forward into a front line. Kutuzov was unaware of this change to the intended plan, presumed that it originated with Tuchkov (who was killed in the battle and thus could not explain), and was suitably angry with Bennigsen when the facts became known.

The next day, 6 September, passed without action, as Napoleon prepared his army for battle. The Russian right, shielded by the Kolotcha, was clearly too strong to be attacked; but the left was more vulnerable. Napoleon reconnoitred, and received a proposal from Davout for an audacious manoeuvre: he suggested that his own I Corps, and Poniatowski's V Corps, be sent on a wide flanking movement to encircle the Russian left and fall upon their rear, while Napoleon made a demonstration along their front; it would, said Davout, 'put an end at once to the Russian army, the battle, and the war'. Napoleon considered and replied, 'No! It is too great a movement; it would remove me too far from my object, and make me lose much time.' Davout persisted until Napoleon snapped, 'Ah! You are always for turning the enemy; it is too dangerous a manoeuvre!' whereupon Davout, according to Ségur, 'returned to his post, murmuring against a prudence which he thought unseasonable, and to which he was not accustomed'[21]. (This was another story upon which Gourgaud cast doubts in his strong criticisms of Ségur.) There was some reason for Napoleon's caution, for a wide flank march would be risky, and if discovered might prompt the Russians to withdraw again before the decisive action could be fought; but by declining Davout's reported plan, Napoleon condemned his army to a bloody frontal assault against a resolute enemy. That resolution, indeed, had been exemplified by the fact that no prisoners had been taken at Shevardino.

Napoleon's plans for the battle involved little subtlety. On the extreme right flank, Poniatowski was to advance against the Russian left, but rather than execute an outflanking manoeuvre as suggested by Davout, it was more of an attempt to divert Russian attention from the main assault. On Napoleon's left flank, Eugène's IV Corps, supported by Grouchy's III Cavalry Corps, was to attack and capture the village of Borodino, thus permitting them to cross the Kolotcha and assail the Great Redoubt, while throwing out just enough forces on the extreme left to hold the Russian right in check. Napoleon's main assault was to be made against Kutuzov's left-centre, against the *flèches* and the area between them and the redoubt. Two of Davout's divisions (of Compans and Dessaix) would attack the *flèches*, with a third (Friant) and elements of Murat's reserve cavalry in support. To Davout's left, Ney's III Corps would attempt to break the Russian line in the region of the demolished village of Semenovskaya, while the two remaining divisions of I Corps (Gérand and Morand) would connect the left of Ney's Corps

French infantry advances to the attack in the classic formation of a battalion column with companies arrayed in three ranks. (Print after Raffet)

with Eugène's force. The Imperial Guard and VIII Corps were to form the reserve. Napoleon's army at this stage numbered about 86,000 infantry, 29,500 cavalry and 16,000 artillery and engineers, with 587 guns.

Both sides resorted to a hint of theatricality to bolster the morale of their forces. In the Russian ranks, Orthodox clergy paraded the great icon of the Black Virgin of Smolensk, and Kutuzov issued a proclamation that exhorted his troops to 'fulfil your duties. Think of the sacrifices of your cities to the flames – of your children who implore your protection. Think of your Emperor, your Lord, who regards you as the source of all his strength; and tomorrow, before the sun sets, you will have traced your faith and your allegiance to your Sovereign and Country, in the blood of the aggressor and his hosts.'[22] It served, commented Ségur, 'to give a thorough tincture of fanaticism to their courage. All, even to the meanest soldier, fancied themselves devoted by God himself to the defence of heaven and their consecrated soil.'

Napoleon's equivalent was much less overt and restricted to some of his closest officers and members of the Guard: on that day he had received from Paris a portrait of his infant son, the King of Rome, which he exhibited outside his tent, 'making it shine as a symbol of hope in the midst of imminent peril'. (Less welcome was the arrival from Spain of Marshal Marmont's aide, Colonel Fabvier, bringing news of the French defeat at Salamanca; according to Gourgaud, Napoleon showed such displeasure that Fabvier felt compelled to restore his honour by fighting on foot, as a volunteer, on the following day.) Napoleon also drafted a proclamation that was to be read to the army, which included the statement that 'victory depends on yourselves... it will give us abundance, good winter quarters, and a prompt return to our country! Conduct yourselves as at Austerlitz, at Friedland, at Vitebsk, at Smolensk, that the latest posterity may relate, with pride, your conduct on this day; that they may say of you – He was at the great battle under the walls of Moscow.'[23]

However this heartened the army – Labaume claimed that those who heard it 'were convinced, that imperious necessity imposed on them the law, to conquer or to die' – Napoleon himself was unwell and perhaps depressed.

Ségur stated that recent fatigues and 'so many cares, and his intense and anxious expectation had worn him out; the coldness of the atmosphere had stuck to him; an irritating fever, a dry cough, and excessive thirst consumed him', and he was suffering from a urinary complaint. During a restless night he was heard 'meditating on the vanities of glory. "What is war? A trade of barbarians, the whole art of which consists in being the strongest at a given point!" He then complained of the fickleness of fortune, which, he said, he began to experience.' Such factors were probably the reason why at times during the campaign, including at Borodino, he seems to have been affected by an element of lethargy so different from the activity of previous campaigns. Early on the morning of 7 September, however, Ney reported that the Russians were still in position, and that the army was awaiting the order to attack. Napoleon 'arose, called his officers, and went out, exclaiming, "We have them at last! Forward! Let us go and open the gates of Moscow!"'

THE BATTLE BEGINS

At about 5.30am Napoleon took up his command post by the Shevardino Redoubt. The sun rose, and Napoleon exclaimed, 'Behold the sun of Austerlitz!'; but, Ségur noted wryly, it rose behind the Russian lines, illuminated Napoleon's position and dazzled his troops. It was, perhaps, an augury of what was to occur during the day.

Throughout the night Napoleon's army had constructed three huge artillery batteries, each of 24 12-pdrs, directed against the Great Redoubt and its environs and against the *flèches*, but daylight revealed that they had been placed out of range of the enemy, so there was a delay while the guns were re-positioned, and it was 6.00am before the cannonade began. The Russians replied, and the bombardment continued, with the exposed

Polish infantry advances: such troops comprised Poniatowski's V Corps and were engaged in the fighting around Utitsa on the Russian left flank. (Print after Raffet)

dispositions of the Russian army leading to heavy casualties, the troops under fire standing stoically while they were shot down. Such was the ferocity of the bombardment that General Nikolai Lavrov, commander of the Lifeguard infantry of V Corps, suffered a nervous collapse.

The first of Napoleon's attacks was mounted by elements of Eugène's IV Corps against the village of Borodino. Despite being on the 'wrong' side of the Kolotcha, and thus somewhat isolated, Kutuzov and Bennigsen had garrisoned the village with the Lifeguard Jägers, to Barclay's dismay; and when the first attack was reported, he ordered them to withdraw. He was too late: Delzons' Division, leading the advance, hurried them over the bridge across the Kolotcha, causing severe casualties. The leading French regiment, the 106th Line, pursued too quickly, crossed the river in disorder and as one of the brigade commanders, General Louis-Auguste Plauzonne, attempted to recall them he was shot dead, the first of Napoleon's senior officers to lose his life in the action. (He had only recently taken command of his brigade; its original leader, General Jean-Claude Roussel, had been mistakenly shot dead by one of his own sentries on 26 July.) Counterattacked, the 106th was bundled back over the river, covered by the 96th Line; but the Russians made no attempt to follow or to recapture Borodino, but just burned the bridge. Eugène retained just enough troops in the area of the village to secure the position – Delzons' Division with cavalry support – and established a 28-gun battery nearby, able to play upon the Great Redoubt and upon the Russian artillery near Gorki.

With the fight begun at Borodino village, Napoleon presumed that his planned move against the Russian left would be under way, with Poniatowski advancing along the Old Smolensk Road, and so initiated the next stage of his plan, an assault by Davout's I Corps against the *flèches*. It was led by the division of General Compans, supported by that of General Joseph-Marie Dessaix. Compans planned an attack in two columns, one to clear the Russian skirmishers from the woodland south of the *flèches* and the other to take the southernmost fortification, but as they advanced – themselves without firing – they came under a hail of artillery fire and musketry, as Ségur described: 'Suddenly, from that peaceful plain, and the silent hills, volumes of fire and smoke were seen spouting out, followed by a multitude of explosions, and the whistling of bullets tearing the air in every direction.' As the advancing troops were lashed by this shot, Compans was hit in the shoulder and put out of action, and Davout was stunned when his horse was shot beneath him, knocking his pistol-holster into him and causing a severe bruise. Initially it was reported to Napoleon that Davout was dead, and the emperor expressed great relief when he discovered that this was not so. Despite the volume of fire coming from the Russian 11th and 32nd Artillery Companies in front of the *flèches*, the attack pressed on and the French 57th Line stormed into the southernmost *flèche*. A counterattack by General Mikhail Vorontsov's 2nd Combined Grenadier Division threw them out again; Sievers's cavalry (14th Brigade plus the New Russia Dragoons) pursued and overran some French guns.

After Compans's injury, General Joseph-Marie Dessaix moved up to command the fight in advance of his own division, but Napoleon sent his own aide, General Jean Rapp, to take over. He immediately conferred with Ney, on the left, to coordinate the attack, as Dessaix's division moved up to bring respite to Compans's battered command. General Francois Ledru des Essarts's 10th Division from Ney's corps attacked what they believed to be the northernmost *flèche* (initially they were unaware that there were three). As the pressure increased on the Russians, Vorontsov's men were reinforced:

Tuchkov, not yet engaged himself, sent north his 3rd Division under General Pyotr Konovnitsyn, while Kutuzov ordered Constantine to send from his reserve the 1st (Lifeguard) Cuirassier Division, infantry and artillery. Until they arrived, Vorontsov's grenadiers had to hold the position. Already lightly wounded, as he headed the 61st Line Rapp was hit in the left hip and thrown from his horse. Dessaix again took over, but almost immediately had his left arm broken by a grapeshot. As Rapp was being treated for his wound, Napoleon visited him to ask how the battle progressed; Rapp replied that 'I believe that you will be obliged to make your guard charge'. Napoleon said, 'I shall take good care not to do so. I do not wish to see it destroyed'[24].

The fighting around the *flèches* was very confused as charge and counter-charge flowed around the fieldworks. The attack mounted by Ledru, with the French 57th Line from Compans's Division, overran their target *flèche*, only to be driven out again; by this time elements of Junot's VIII Corps were in support, and on the Russian side Neverovski's 27th Division, and the 12th Division from Raevski's corps, had been fed into the fight. In response to the recapture of the southern *flèche* Murat, whose cavalry was in support, personally organized a counterattack by the 1st Württemberg Jägers from Marchand's 25th Division of Ney's corps, and the French 72nd Line from Ledru's division, which reoccupied the position once again; but when charged by Russian cuirassiers Murat was forced to seek sanctuary among the Jägers, encouraging them to hold firm until the remainder of the Württembergers came up in support.

Murat at the *flèches*; as Russian cuirassiers counterattacked he had to seek refuge among the Württembergers of Marchand's 25th Division. He is shown here, centre, on the white horse. (Print after Christian Faber du Faur)

THE RUSSIAN LEFT

As the fighting raged around the *flèches*, pressure began to be applied to the Russian left wing. Poniatowski's movement against the Russian flank had begun at daybreak, but it was not until about 8.00am that V Corps came into action against Tuchkov's III Corps, already weakened by the despatch of troops to support the defenders of the *flèches*. Poniatowski ran into Tuchkov's first line, elements of General P. A. Stroganov's 1st Grenadier Division, which was ordered to burn Utitsa village and fall back. Poniatowski paused to reorganize,

MURAT AT BORODINO (pp. 50–51)

As in every action, Murat was in the forefront of the battle at Borodino, heedless of danger. Louis Lejeune, carrying a message to him from Napoleon, found him amid a skirmish-line, well in advance of his own cavalry. Nearby Cossacks had recognized him from his flamboyant costume and his distinctive long hair, and were shouting 'Houra! Houra! Murat!', as much in admiration as with hostile intent; for, recalled Lejeune, none dare approach him for reason of his reputation as a swordsman. This depicts another noted incident involving the marshal, when Murat **(1)** took shelter among the members of Marchand's 25th (Württemberg) Division **(2)** that was fighting for possession of the *flèches*. He rode among them to encourage them – he is seen here, in his eccentric uniform, exhorting the Württemberg Jägers – as they were charged by Russian cuirassiers **(3)** who, one witness thought, were at first mistaken for Saxon cavalry because of the similarity of uniform (both wore white, which could be confused amid the smoke of battle). The Jägers held off the Russian cavalry until other Württemberg infantry came up in support; they are seen here **(4)**, behind the green-clad Jägers, distinguished by their crested leather helmets.

and at about 10.30am recommenced his advance, having assembled a 22-gun battery to pound the Utitsa mound, upon which the Russians had installed four 12-pdrs. The odds were heavily against the Russians at this point, and reinforcement was essential. Realizing the danger, Kutuzov and Barclay ordered Baggovut, whose II Corps was unoccupied on the extreme right flank, to send one of his divisions (the 17th) to the other flank, marching in the rear of the Russian front line, and as the full nature of the threat became evident, his other division (the 4th) was ordered to follow, leaving just his Jäger regiments to continue to hold the right flank.

Baggovut's men made their march, north to south behind the front line, at maximum speed; but by that stage the fighting along the centre and left was so fierce that he had to drop off units to assist as he marched past: Eugen of Württemberg, two regiments from the 17th Division and part of the 17th Artillery Company. At Tuchkov's request, Baggovut hurried forward two regiments (Belozersk and Wilmanstrand) and the remaining six guns of the 17th Artillery Company to provide immediate support to the hard-pressed left flank. Tuchkov directed them to the Utitsa mound, but they were out-gunned by Poniatowski's battery, and had to relinquish that position; but when the remainder of II Corps came up the Russians counterattacked and repossessed Utitsa village. Tuchkov was mortally wounded leading the Pavlov Grenadier Regiment of Stroganov's Division, and command of the Russian left devolved upon Baggovut.

General Louis-Pierre Montbrun (1770–1812), commander of II Cavalry Corps; he was mortally wounded by a shell fragment before the great cavalry attack on the Russian centre. Marbot described him as 'a splendid man, in the same style as Murat'. (Print by Forestier)

THE CENTRE

The need to reinforce the Russian left deprived the centre of some possible support. The fight around the *flèches* continued, the second of Napoleon's major attacks lasting more than two hours, with Friant's 2nd Division of Davout's I Corps being employed in assisting Ney; in all Napoleon committed about 45,000 men to this sector of the battle. Attack after attack was hurled against the positions, with the Russians counterattacking with vigour, and apart from the close-quarter infantry combat the artillery bombardment was immense, Napoleon deploying about 400 guns and the Russians about 300 in this sector. It was this torrent of fire that, some time before 10.00am, accounted for the most high-profile casualty of the battle: Bagration, in the thick of the action, was hit in the leg and was unable to continue in command. To the dismay of his troops, to whom he was an inspiration and a hero, he was borne away; the wound was to prove fatal, and he died on 24 September. Command of the sector passed to Konovnitsyn and, primarily, to Dokhturov; but with the fighting further north along the Russian line at a desperate stage so as to prevent further reinforcement, they were unable to hold the fortifications, despite the *flèches* having been retaken several times. The Russians pulled back, leaving them in the possession of the enemy.

While the fight for the *flèches* was proceeding, Napoleon's army made its attack upon the salient point of the Russian centre, the Great Redoubt. Leaving Delzons' Division to garrison Borodino village, Eugène brought his 14th Division (General Jean-Baptiste Broussier) with the 1st (Morand) and 3rd (Gerard) of Davout's corps, over the Kolotcha by means of pontoon bridging, but the initial lack of urgency caused the Russians to suspect it was a diversionary movement, so that their position at the Redoubt was not as reinforced as otherwise it might have been, and indeed Raevski's command

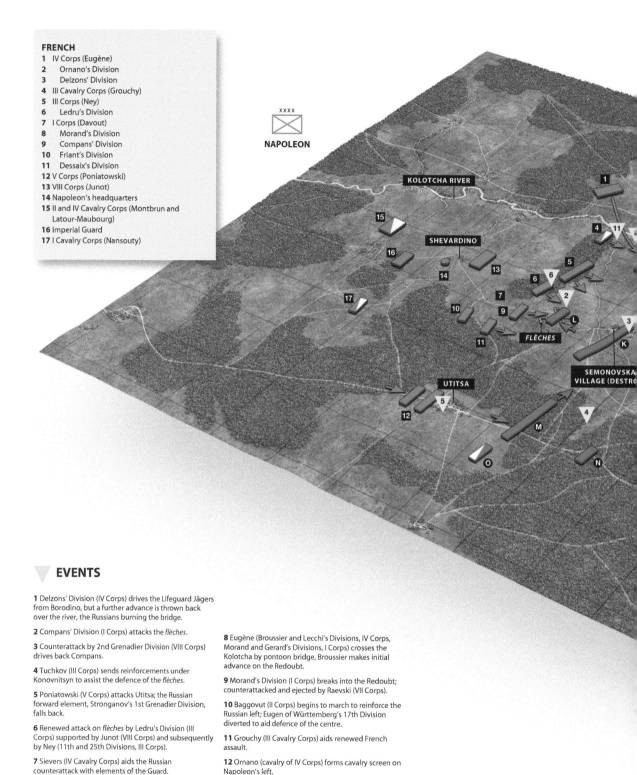

FRENCH
1 IV Corps (Eugène)
2   Ornano's Division
3   Delzons' Division
4 III Cavalry Corps (Grouchy)
5 III Corps (Ney)
6   Ledru's Division
7 I Corps (Davout)
8   Morand's Division
9   Compans' Division
10   Friant's Division
11   Dessaix's Division
12 V Corps (Poniatowski)
13 VIII Corps (Junot)
14 Napoleon's headquarters
15 II and IV Cavalry Corps (Montbrun and
     Latour-Maubourg)
16 Imperial Guard
17 I Cavalry Corps (Nansouty)

xxxx
NAPOLEON

KOLOTCHA RIVER

SHEVARDINO

FLÈCHES

UTITSA

SEMONOVSKA
VILLAGE (DESTRO

▼ EVENTS

1 Delzons' Division (IV Corps) drives the Lifeguard Jägers from Borodino, but a further advance is thrown back over the river, the Russians burning the bridge.

2 Compans' Division (I Corps) attacks the *flèches*.

3 Counterattack by 2nd Grenadier Division (VIII Corps) drives back Compans.

4 Tuchkov (III Corps) sends reinforcements under Konovnitsyn to assist the defence of the *flèches*.

5 Poniatowski (V Corps) attacks Utitsa; the Russian forward element, Stronganov's 1st Grenadier Division, falls back.

6 Renewed attack on *flèches* by Ledru's Division (III Corps) supported by Junot (VIII Corps) and subsequently by Ney (11th and 25th Divisions, III Corps).

7 Sievers (IV Cavalry Corps) aids the Russian counterattack with elements of the Guard.

8 Eugène (Broussier and Lecchi's Divisions, IV Corps, Morand and Gerard's Divisions, I Corps) crosses the Kolotcha by pontoon bridge, Broussier makes initial advance on the Redoubt.

9 Morand's Division (I Corps) breaks into the Redoubt; counterattacked and ejected by Raevski (VII Corps).

10 Baggovut (II Corps) begins to march to reinforce the Russian left; Eugen of Württemberg's 17th Division diverted to aid defence of the centre.

11 Grouchy (III Cavalry Corps) aids renewed French assault.

12 Ornano (cavalry of IV Corps) forms cavalry screen on Napoleon's left.

BORODINO TO ABOUT 1000HRS, 7 SEPTEMBER
The Grande Armée attacks the *flèches*.

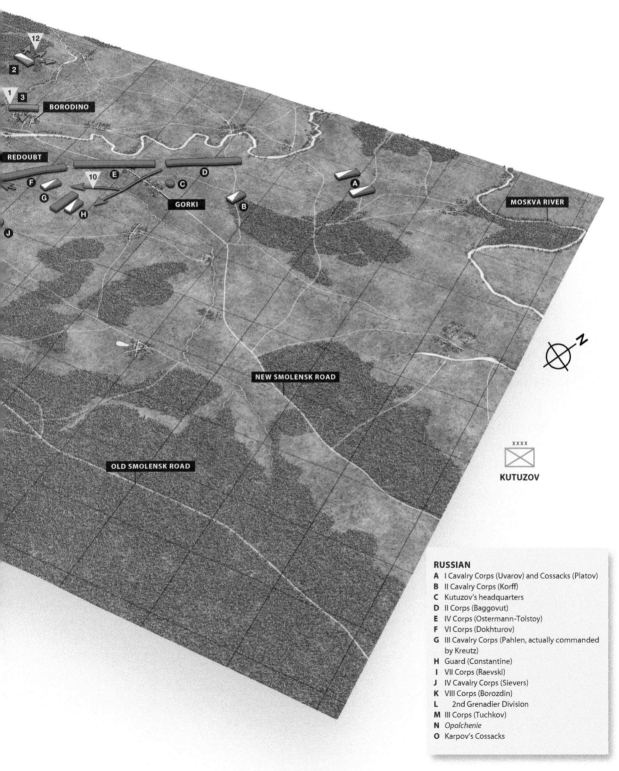

BORODINO

REDOUBT

MOSKVA RIVER

GORKI

NEW SMOLENSK ROAD

OLD SMOLENSK ROAD

xxxx

KUTUZOV

RUSSIAN
A I Cavalry Corps (Uvarov) and Cossacks (Platov)
B II Cavalry Corps (Korff)
C Kutuzov's headquarters
D II Corps (Baggovut)
E IV Corps (Ostermann-Tolstoy)
F VI Corps (Dokhturov)
G III Cavalry Corps (Pahlen, actually commanded by Kreutz)
H Guard (Constantine)
I VII Corps (Raevski)
J IV Cavalry Corps (Sievers)
K VIII Corps (Borozdin)
L   2nd Grenadier Division
M III Corps (Tuchkov)
N Opolchenie
O Karpov's Cossacks

had already been weakened in support of Tuchkov. Raevski – somewhat immobile following a recent injury – stationed himself in the midst of the defences, and threw out a strong skirmish-line of not only his own Jäger regiments but also the 18th Jägers from IV Corps and the 40th from VI Corps. The Redoubt itself was held by the 26th Artillery Brigade, and in the rear the 19th Jägers (from VI Corps) and Raevski's own two divisions, Vasil'chikov's 12th on the left and Paskevich's 26th on the right.

Eugène began his attack with a huge bombardment – Kreutz's Russian III Cavalry Corps in the rear was especially mauled by it – and at about 10.00am Broussier's Division moved towards the north-west front of the Redoubt, and was beaten off. It was clearly only a precursor for a more sustained attack, so that when Konovnitsyn informed Raevski of Bagration's injury, with the implication that Raevski should take command of the left, he felt unable to leave his post. Almost immediately, however, he had to be hustled out of the Redoubt to safety as French troops poured in. Approaching from the south-west, the attack was mounted by Morand's Division, of which the 30th Line rushed the earthworks and entered through the embrasures, led by their brigade commander, General Charles-Auguste Bonnamy. They had a hand-to-hand fight with the Russian gunners, but not only threw them out but advanced some 50 metres (160ft) beyond the Redoubt. The remainder of Morand's Division, however, with the exception of a battalion of the 13th Light, was too heavily engaged outside the earthwork to come to their support.

Their possession of the Redoubt was fleeting. Raevski had posted his two divisions at the rear to facilitate a counter-attack, and this was launched without delay, the 12th and 26th Divisions being joined by elements from General Pyotr Likachev's 24th Division of VI Corps. These were directed to the fight by two of Barclay's staff officers, his aide Waldemar von Löwenstern and his chief of staff General Alexei Ermolov, who saw Raevski's Jägers falling back in complete disorder. Attacked from three sides, the 30th Line was decimated and bundled back out of the Redoubt; Bonnamy received between 15 and 20 wounds before he was captured and taken to Kutuzov, who had his injuries treated. Bonnamy survived to remain in captivity until 1814. In this stage of the action the Russians suffered a great loss: the artillery commander General Alexander Kutaisov, a very capable and esteemed officer but perhaps too brave for his own good, became involved in the counterattack and was killed, his death leading to the artillery not being deployed as it might.

As Bonnamy would have discovered, Kutuzov remained at his headquarters at Gorki throughout the battle; thus he had no personal observation of the unfolding events, relying upon messengers from the battle-front and upon the suggestions of others. He was not entirely inactive, but appeared to contribute little beyond the acceptance of suggestions put to him. Clausewitz saw him during the battle, and although he admitted that it was a relatively fleeting glimpse, the opinions he gathered from others matched his own: 'he was almost a nullity. He appeared destitute of inward activity, or any clear view of surrounding occurrences, of any liveliness of perception, of independence of action. He suffered the subordinate directors of the contest to take their own course, and appeared to be for the individual transactions of the day nothing but an abstract idea of a central authority.' His value, however, was greater as a strategist and figurehead: Bagration had been present in the line-of-battle and Russia had lost him as a consequence. Clausewitz thought that Kutuzov's 'discharge of this great function was anything but brilliant', but acknowledged that 'cunning and prudence... adhered to Kutuzov; and with these he overlooked his own position and that of his adversary better than Barclay with his limited mental vision'[25]. It was, perhaps, also fortunate for the Russians that Napoleon also exhibited at Borodino much less activity than he had on many previous occasions.

The fighting slackened temporarily, the French artillery afraid of hitting their own retiring troops, until a new attack was made. As Baggovut's Corps was making its march from the north to bolster the left wing, Eugen of Württemberg was with it, to the rear of the Redoubt, when a cloud of dust swept down upon it, heralding a cavalry charge. Grouchy's III Cavalry Corps fell upon them, but the Russians formed square and resisted – sheltering Barclay and Raevski among others – and the cavalry drew back. Napoleon's artillery increased its bombardment – Eugen of Württemberg had three horses shot from beneath him and had to mount an artillery horse – and Ermolov was put out of action by a canister shot in the neck; but the Redoubt remained in Russian hands.

General Emmanuel Grouchy (1766–1847), commander of III Cavalry Corps at Borodino, where he was wounded in the breast by a grapeshot.

SEMENOVSKAYA

Between the Great Redoubt and the *flèches* lay that part of the Russian line forward of the demolished village of Semenovskaya. The line consisted primarily of Vorontsov's 2nd Combined Grenadier Division, and on their left flank the three Lifeguard regiments Ismailovski, Litovski and Finland, with the 1st Cuirassier Division in support (also Lifeguard regiments), and all from the reserve. Konovnitsyn's 3rd Division, involved in the fight for the *flèches*, was also in reserve, as was Sievers's IV Cavalry Corps on the right. Against this sector of the Russian line, Napoleon deployed the one division of Davout's corps not already engaged, General Louis Friant's 2nd Division, with General Etienne-Marie Nansouty's I Cavalry Corps on its right and General Marie-Victor Latour-Maubourg's IV Cavalry Corps on its left. Murat was present to direct the attack.

Preparations for the assault had begun at about 7.00am, but it was about 10.00am before the troops moved into the attack, preceded by the usual

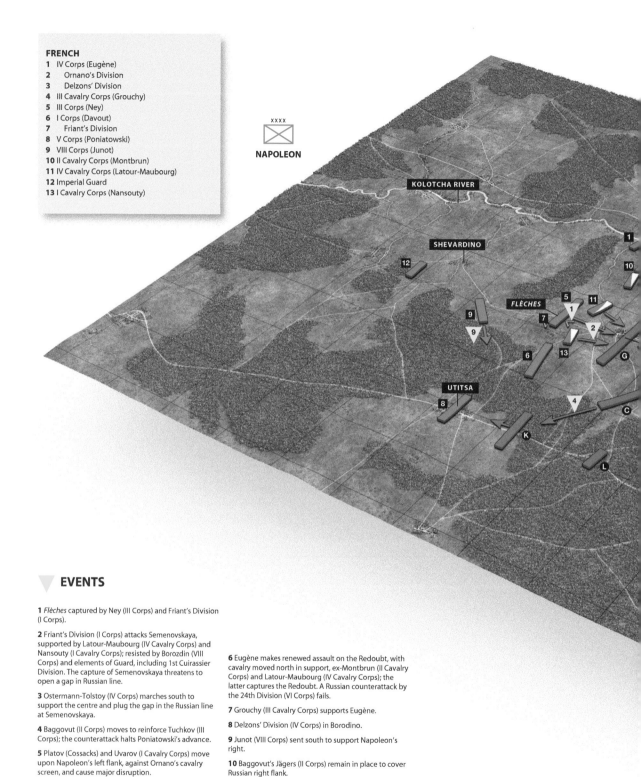

FRENCH
1. IV Corps (Eugène)
2. Ornano's Division
3. Delzons' Division
4. III Cavalry Corps (Grouchy)
5. III Corps (Ney)
6. I Corps (Davout)
7. Friant's Division
8. V Corps (Poniatowski)
9. VIII Corps (Junot)
10. II Cavalry Corps (Montbrun)
11. IV Cavalry Corps (Latour-Maubourg)
12. Imperial Guard
13. I Cavalry Corps (Nansouty)

xxxx
NAPOLEON

KOLOTCHA RIVER

SHEVARDINO

FLÈCHES

UTITSA

▼ EVENTS

1 *Flèches* captured by Ney (III Corps) and Friant's Division (I Corps).

2 Friant's Division (I Corps) attacks Semenovskaya, supported by Latour-Maubourg (IV Cavalry Corps) and Nansouty (I Cavalry Corps); resisted by Borozdin (VIII Corps) and elements of Guard, including 1st Cuirassier Division. The capture of Semenovskaya threatens to open a gap in Russian line.

3 Ostermann-Tolstoy (IV Corps) marches south to support the centre and plug the gap in the Russian line at Semenovskaya.

4 Baggovut (II Corps) moves to reinforce Tuchkov (III Corps); the counterattack halts Poniatowski's advance.

5 Platov (Cossacks) and Uvarov (I Cavalry Corps) move upon Napoleon's left flank, against Ornano's cavalry screen, and cause major disruption.

6 Eugène makes renewed assault on the Redoubt, with cavalry moved north in support, ex-Montbrun (II Cavalry Corps) and Latour-Maubourg (IV Cavalry Corps); the latter captures the Redoubt. A Russian counterattack by the 24th Division (VI Corps) fails.

7 Grouchy (III Cavalry Corps) supports Eugène.

8 Delzons' Division (IV Corps) in Borodino.

9 Junot (VIII Corps) sent south to support Napoleon's right.

10 Baggovut's Jägers (II Corps) remain in place to cover Russian right flank.

BORODINO, ACTION TO ABOUT 1500HRS, 7 SEPTEMBER
The fight for Semonovskaya and the Great Redoubt.

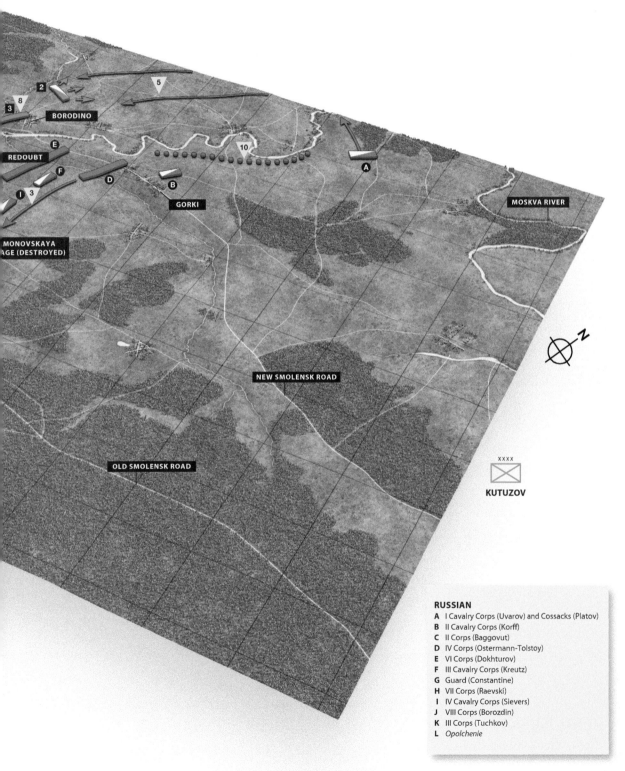

Note: Gridlines are shown at intervals of 1km/0.62miles

2

5

3 8

BORODINO

E

REDOUBT

F

D

10

I 3

B

A

GORKI

MONOVSKAYA
AGE (DESTROYED)

MOSKVA RIVER

N

NEW SMOLENSK ROAD

xxxx

OLD SMOLENSK ROAD

KUTUZOV

RUSSIAN
A I Cavalry Corps (Uvarov) and Cossacks (Platov)
B II Cavalry Corps (Korff)
C II Corps (Baggovut)
D IV Corps (Ostermann-Tolstoy)
E VI Corps (Dokhturov)
F III Cavalry Corps (Kreutz)
G Guard (Constantine)
H VII Corps (Raevski)
I IV Cavalry Corps (Sievers)
J VIII Corps (Borozdin)
K III Corps (Tuchkov)
L *Opolchenie*

The attack on the Great Redoubt: French cuirassiers charge the position. (Print after Albrecht Adam)

massive artillery bombardment. North of the village, Latour-Maubourg's two divisions (4th Light and 7th Cuirassier) assailed the 2nd Combined Grenadiers as they were in process of forming square, rode some down and went on to the north and rear of the village, where they were counter-charged by Sievers's IV Cavalry Corps. The 7th Cuirassier Division was formed of troops from the Confederation of the Rhine: the 14th Polish Cuirassiers, the two Saxon heavy regiments (Garde du Corps and Zastrow Cuirassiers) and the two Westphalian cuirassier regiments; at first the Russians disordered the leading elements, but the arrival of the Westphalian cuirassiers drove the Russians away, and Latour-Maubourg's men clung to the area to the north of the village.

To the south, Nansouty's corps met with less success; they were unable to break the Lifeguard infantry, among the elite of the Russian army, and in one instance the Litovski Regiment actually mounted a bayonet-charge against the French cavalry; and a Russian cavalry counter-charge stabilized their situation. Between the two cavalry actions, Friant's infantry advanced against the 2nd Combined Grenadier Division, Dokhturov being on hand to supervise the Russian defence. He moved up the Moscow and Astrakhan Grenadier Regiments (from VIII Corps) but they were unable to prevent the French from breaching the line, led by General François-Marie Dufour at the head of the 15th Light. The Russians continued to throw in a storm of fire, which led to an exchange recounted by Ségur. One of the French unit-commanders gave orders to pull back out of the lashing shot; 'Murat ran up to him, and seizing him by the collar, exclaimed, "What are you about?" The colonel, pointing to the ground, covered with half his troops, answered, "You see well enough that it is impossible to stand here." "Very well, I will remain!" exclaimed the king [Murat]. These words stopped the officer: he looked Murat steadily in the face, and turning round, coolly said, "You are right! Soldiers, face to the enemy! Let us go and get killed!"'[26] (This was another story denied, perhaps not very convincingly, by Gourgaud in his condemnation of Ségur's account:

he stated that in the entire army there was not one commanding officer who needed to be reminded of his duty.)

As the fighting raged, Murat sent his deputy chief of staff, Adjutant-Commandant Charles-Luc Borrelli, to seek reinforcements. He found Napoleon at his headquarters, seated on a chair and apparently in a state of lethargy. Napoleon agreed to Borrelli's appeal and ordered the advance of the Young Guard; but countermanded the order almost immediately. Its commander, the comte de Lobau (General Georges Mouton), presumably anxious to join the battle, continued to advance little by little under the pretence of dressing the line; but when Napoleon noticed it he repeated the order to halt. Murat next sent his chief of staff, General Auguste-Daniel Belliard, to repeat the plea for support; this was also denied. Sent back to report on the progress of the action, Belliard returned to Napoleon with information that the Russians appeared to be forming a new line to the rear of their original position and that it was imperative that a new assault be ordered, implying the use of the Imperial Guard. According to Ségur, Napoleon replied, '"that nothing was yet sufficiently unravelled: that to make him give his reserves, he wanted to see more clearly upon his chess-board". This was his expression, which he repeated several times, at the same time pointing to the great redoubt.'

Belliard reported back to Murat and Ney, observing that he had found Napoleon 'still seated in the same place, with a suffering and dejected air, his features sunk, and a dull look; giving his orders languishingly, in the midst of these dreadful warlike noises, to which he seemed completely a stranger'. Murat, realizing from the previous day that Napoleon had seemed unwell, reacted with equanimity, but the more choleric Ney burst out, 'What business has the emperor in the rear of the army? There he is only within reach of reverse and not of victory. Since he will no longer make war himself, since his is no longer the general, as he wishes to be the emperor every where, let him return to the Tuileries, and leave us to be general for him!' Others of Napoleon's staff continued to urge that the Guard be committed to turn the battle, but Napoleon replied, 'And if there should be another battle tomorrow, where is my army?'

The re-forming Russian line behind Semenovskaya reported to Napoleon was the consequence of a continuing process of the transfer of resources from the unengaged Russian right flank: Ostermann-Tolstoy's IV Corps was marched south from its original position in the line to shore up the centre. This movement, essentially defensive, was viewed as a sufficient threat to persuade Napoleon to commit one element of the Guard, General Jean-Barthelemot Sorbier's 60 guns of the Guard Artillery, in support of Friant; they opened a bombardment that lashed Ostermann-Tolstoy's men, but stoically they remained in position, closing up to fill the gaps blasted through their lines. Their presence was needed as the Russian defenders of the *flèches* relinquished the position and fell back beyond the Semenovka stream.

THE RUSSIAN RIGHT WING

The Russian centre, anchored on the Great Redoubt, still held firm, and a renewed assault upon it was considerably delayed. Part of the reason, and to Napoleon confirmation that he was right in holding back the Imperial Guard, were events unfolding upon his extreme left wing. Kutuzov's far right was held by a skirmish-screen of Cossacks led by their Hetman, Matvei Platov. Early in the morning he had observed that the Grande Armée had left the banks of the Kolotcha, far to the north-east of Borodino, virtually unguarded, with their left flank protected by just a cavalry screen from Eugène's corps, the light brigades under the overall command of Napoleon's cousin, General Philippe-Antoine Ornano. Sensing the possibilities, Platov sent an aide to Kutuzov – intercepted by Toll – to suggest that a cavalry force should turn Napoleon's left flank and fall on his rear. Toll approved and proposed that all the Russian right-wing cavalry be used; Kutuzov assented, and so not only Platov's 5,500 Cossacks but the 2,500 regulars of General Feodor Uvarov's I Cavalry Corps were ordered into action. At about 11.00am Platov and Uvarov forded the Kolotcha and made a wide outflanking manoeuvre to the north of Borodino village, pushing aside Ornano's outposts. The Cossacks ranged further west, but Uvarov's cavalry was checked by Delzons' Division, which had moved to the north of Borodino, and most of Grouchy's III Cavalry Corps also moved northwards against the Russians. Unable to make any further progress, the Russian cavalry was ordered to retire at about 3.00pm and fell back upon the Kolotcha, crossing the river again onto the east bank and forming to the rear of Gorki between 4.00 and 5.00pm. Clausewitz – Uvarov's quartermaster-general – was present, and thought the enterprise doomed from the beginning, as Uvarov had only 12 guns and no infantry, making it impossible to break into Borodino, while 'so many troops were seen standing idle as reserves on the other side, that it was plainly impossible for 2500 horse to affect the result of the battle by any effort in that quarter'.

The Redoubt: Napoleon's cuirassiers attempt to gain entry, while Auguste de Caulaincourt falls mortally wounded. (Print by Audibon after Raffet)

The Russian command was desperately disappointed with both Uvarov and Platov (though in fairness to the latter it was acknowledged that Cossacks were of limited use in a conventional battle); but the true influence of Uvarov's manoeuvre was actually exemplified by Clausewitz's remark concerning the large numbers of enemy troops assembled to oppose them. In fact, Uvarov's diversion was a crucial manoeuvre, for its threat caused great consternation among the Grande Armée, serving to paralyse Napoleon's left for some hours, and pulling away troops, including Grouchy's cavalry, from the centre. It also seems likely that it delayed the next attack on the Russian centre, buying precious time for the reorganization of their line.

THE FALL OF THE GREAT REDOUBT

Despite much of Napoleon's army being distracted by Uvarov and Platov, action along the Russian line did not cease, although for a period it consisted largely of exchanges of artillery fire. Murat's cavalry, deployed motionless within range of the Russian guns, suffered especially. Ségur stated that Murat complained to Napoleon about the losses he was sustaining, and requested that the cavalry of the Imperial Guard be sent to join him in an attack. Napoleon seemed to consent and sent for the commander of the Guard cavalry, Marshal Jean-Baptiste Bessières, but it was almost an hour before he could be found, and the moment was lost. Among the casualties incurred by the Russian artillery was the charismatic commander of II Cavalry Corps, General Louis-Pierre Montbrun, who was mortally hit by a shell splinter. To replace him Napoleon sent one of his own aides, General Auguste-Jean de Caulaincourt, younger brother of Napoleon's principal diplomatic advisor, General Armand-Auguste de Caulaincourt, who was at Napoleon's side during the battle. The younger Caulaincourt arrived at his temporary command to find Montbrun's officers in tears at their leader's fall; Caulaincourt told them, 'weep not for him, but come and avenge his death!'

Just before 3.00pm another great attack was mounted on the Redoubt. Eugène was there in person, exhorting each regiment as it passed: 'Remember, your reputation depends on this day!'; to the 9th Line, 'Remember you were with me at Wagram, when we broke the enemy's centre'. Eugène's attack comprised three infantry divisions (Broussier's from his own IV Corps, Gerard's and Morand's from I Corps), with on their right Caulaincourt and II Cavalry Corps, and the south Latour-Maubourg's IV Cavalry Corps. Recognizing the preparation for an assault, Barclay ordered up his 1st Cuirassier Division in support, but they had moved towards the left flank and only a few cavalry elements were immediately to hand. As Eugène's advance began, the cavalry quickly outpaced the infantry and aimed to turn the flanks of the Redoubt and take it in the rear. When he received the order to advance on the fortification, Caulaincourt replied that, 'You shall see me there presently, dead or alive', and as he led the 5th Cuirassiers of Watier's Division he was shot dead by a musket ball. Watier's troopers were turned back by the volume of fire, but the 7th Cuirassier Division of IV Cavalry Corps, the Saxon Garde du Corps and Zastrow Cuirassiers, and the 14th Polish Cuirassiers, surged around the left flank of the Redoubt and overran it, riding on into the hollow behind the fortification where they encountered the principal Russian defenders, the 7th and 24th Divisions of Dokhturov's Corps.

Behind the firing-line at Borodino, a scene observed by Albrecht Adam: the death of the Bavarian cavalry colonel Count Wittgenstein, mortally wounded by a roundshot. The wounded cuirassier leaving the field at the right is from the French 10th Cuirassiers of Watier's division of Montbrun's II Cavalry Corps.

The capture of such a position by cavalry alone was an almost unprecedented feat. Eugène followed the cavalry with his infantry, Broussier in the lead with Morand in support, and was, as described by Ségur, 'on the point of reaching the mouth of this volcano, when suddenly he saw its fires extinguished, its smoke disappear, and its summit glittering with the moveable and resplendent armour of our cuirassiers'[27]. Surging into the Redoubt, they found a scene of carnage, the Russian gunners having fought to the last: 'The interior of the redoubt presented a horrid picture to our sight. The dead were heaped on one another, from among which the cries of the wounded were feebly heard... the parapets, half demolished, had the embrasures entirely destroyed, and their places were distinguished but by the cannon, the greatest part of which were thrown down, and separated from their broken carriages'[28]; yet still the Russians had been able to rescue six of their guns before they were overrun.

News of the capture of the Redoubt was conveyed to Napoleon, and of Caulaincourt's death. His brother Armand was at Napoleon's side; he remained impassive but for tears running down his cheeks. Seeing his distress Napoleon asked if he wished to retire; but Caulaincourt merely half raised his hat as a gesture of thanks and stuck to his post.

Barclay was not prepared to accept the fall of the Redoubt without a further effort, and fed in his own cavalry: at first the Lifeguard, followed by II and III Cavalry Corps, while Eugène consolidated possession of the Redoubt with his infantry, and brought up the cavalry within range, including Grouchy's III Cavalry Corps. They engaged the Russians on the plateau behind the Redoubt in a protracted and confused cavalry fight that lasted for as long as two hours, the Russian infantry forming square and driving off those who charged them.

THE BATTLE ENDS

Learning of the fall of the Great Redoubt, on the Russian left flank Poniatowski made a renewed effort, attacking with a column on either side of the Utitsa mound. The assault to the north of the mound stalled, but that to the south drove on, until stopped by a desperate counterattack mounted by Baggovut, involving the 1st Grenadier and 17th Divisions. Dangerously exposed by events further north, Baggovut decided it necessary to pull back his line along the Old Smolensk Road, but gave Eugen of Württemberg permission to make a final attempt to recover the area around the Utitsa mound. He led what remained of the Kremenchug and Minsk Regiments from his own 4th Division, but they numbered only about 500–600 men, and were forced to retire with heavy losses.

The fighting to the rear of the Redoubt, and elsewhere along the line, began to abate from the sheer exhaustion of both sides. Clausewitz described the Russian perspective:

> We looked at the battle; and we still have in our recollection the character of weariness and exhaustion which it assumed. The infantry masses were so reduced, that, perhaps, not more than a third of their original strength was engaged. The rest were either killed, wounded, engaged in removing the wounded, or rallying in the rear. Large vacancies were everywhere apparent. That enormous artillery... was now heard only in single shots, and even these seemed to have lost the thunder of their original voice, and to give a hoarse and hollow tone. The cavalry had almost everywhere taken up the place and position of the infantry, and made its attacks in a weary trot.

On the field of Borodino: Russian prisoners under guard, including a hussar (left) and a dragoon wearing the distinctive, high-crowned, combed dragoon helmet. (Print after Albrecht Adam)

FALL OF THE GREAT REDOUBT (pp. 66–67)

The final capture of the Great Redoubt was a remarkable feat, accomplished by cavalry before any infantry could arrive in support. The attack against the northern flank and rear of the Redoubt by Watier's French cuirassiers was driven off by musketry from Russian infantry supporting the fortification; it was then that Auguste de Caulaincourt was killed. The troops who actually penetrated the position were the Saxon Garde du Corps and part of the Zastrow Cuirassiers from Lorge's Division, some scrambling through the embrasures or the flanks while others skirted the position to assail the infantry in the rear. In this illustration members of the two Saxon regiments charge into the Redoubt, defended by Russian artillery **(1)**

(26th brigade), and although there was no room in the position for a strong force of infantry, it is likely that some Jägers **(2)** would have joined in the defence. The Saxon regiments both wore combed helmets, the Zastrow Cuirassiers **(3)** with white jackets faced yellow and the Garde du Corps **(4)** straw-yellow faced blue; the former wore their cuirasses, but the latter had left theirs behind at the outset of the campaign, and for protection wore their cloaks in a bulky roll across the chest. When the following infantry broke in to secure the position it was reported that they found the Redoubt piled high with bodies, the Saxons recognizable instantly by their light-coloured uniforms.

At that stage, Clausewitz thought, 'the decision depended entirely on the possession of the last trump card, i.e. the strongest reserve'; but Kutuzov's reserve had already been committed. Napoleon still had the Imperial Guard; but this time Berthier and Murat advised against throwing it into the battle. Gourgaud concurred, describing the Guard as 'like a fortified town, under shelter of which the army might at all times have rallied', emphasizing that as the campaign was not over, its preservation was paramount[29].

As the fighting subsided from the exhaustion of both sides, from right to left the Russians had been driven from their original positions, but still held an improvised line stretching from Gorki in the north to the Old Smolensk Road in the south; the corps were considerably intermingled and many units were shattered to the point of virtual extinction. A member of Barclay's staff, Ludwig von Wolzogen, recalled coming across a Russian lieutenant and 30 or 40 men standing resolutely in the vicinity of the Russian line. Wolzogen ordered him to rejoin his regiment; 'This *is* my regiment' was the reply. When Wolzogen delivered to Kutuzov Barclay's report on the parlous state of the Russian army, Kutuzov seemed to refuse to believe it and even implied that Wolzogen must have been drinking to believe such depressing information. Kutuzov declared that he would hold his ground and attack on the morrow, but Barclay knew the true position: that barely 45,000 men were in any state to fight, and they were exhausted; and that with scant opportunity for resupply, it would be even worse next day. There were conflicting estimates of the Russian loss, though it was somewhere in the region of 40,000 to 44,000.

On Napoleon's side the situation was not much different, though the presence of an uncommitted reserve gave Napoleon a marked advantage. This was perhaps not so obvious when the field was inspected after the fighting subsided. Ségur remarked that:

> The losses were certainly immense, and out of all proportion to the advantage gained. Every one... had to lament the loss of a friend, a relation, or a brother.... Forty-three generals had been killed or wounded.... In [Napoleon's] army, even in his very tent, victory was silent, gloomy, isolated'. A subsequent tour of the

LEFT
The Saxon Zastrow Cuirassiers from Latour-Maubourg's IV Cavalry Corps, heavily engaged in the centre at Borodino. (Print after Charles Rozat de Mandres)

RIGHT
Napoleon's cuirassiers engage the Russian defenders of the Great Redoubt. (Engraving after Horace Vernet)

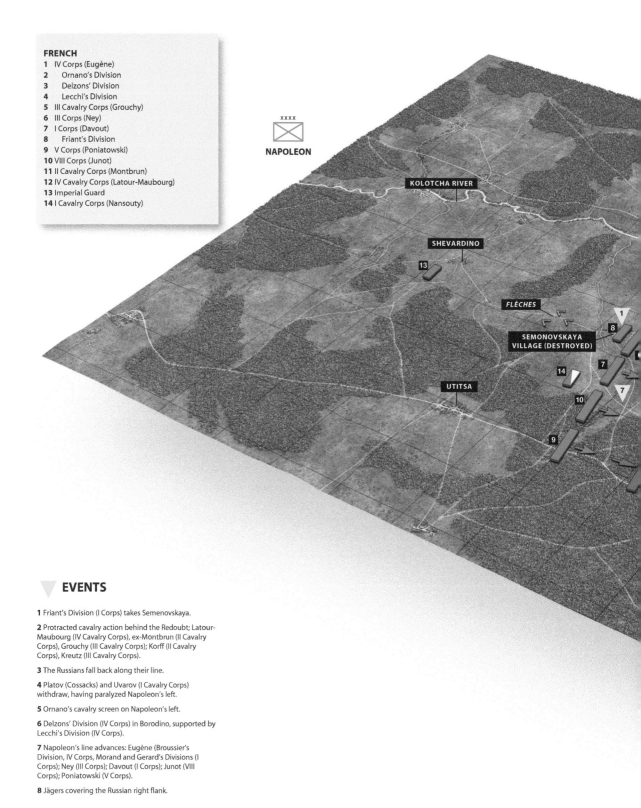

FRENCH

1 IV Corps (Eugène)
2   Ornano's Division
3   Delzons' Division
4   Lecchi's Division
5 III Cavalry Corps (Grouchy)
6 III Corps (Ney)
7 I Corps (Davout)
8   Friant's Division
9 V Corps (Poniatowski)
10 VIII Corps (Junot)
11 II Cavalry Corps (Montbrun)
12 IV Cavalry Corps (Latour-Maubourg)
13 Imperial Guard
14 I Cavalry Corps (Nansouty)

xxxx

NAPOLEON

KOLOTCHA RIVER

SHEVARDINO

FLÈCHES

SEMONOVSKAYA
VILLAGE (DESTROYED)

UTITSA

▼ EVENTS

1 Friant's Division (I Corps) takes Semenovskaya.

2 Protracted cavalry action behind the Redoubt; Latour-Maubourg (IV Cavalry Corps), ex-Montbrun (II Cavalry Corps), Grouchy (III Cavalry Corps); Korff (II Cavalry Corps), Kreutz (III Cavalry Corps).

3 The Russians fall back along their line.

4 Platov (Cossacks) and Uvarov (I Cavalry Corps) withdraw, having paralyzed Napoleon's left.

5 Ornano's cavalry screen on Napoleon's left.

6 Delzons' Division (IV Corps) in Borodino, supported by Lecchi's Division (IV Corps).

7 Napoleon's line advances: Eugène (Broussier's Division, IV Corps, Morand and Gerard's Divisions (I Corps); Ney (III Corps); Davout (I Corps); Junot (VIII Corps); Poniatowski (V Corps).

8 Jägers covering the Russian right flank.

BORODINO, ACTION FROM ABOUT 1500HRS, 7 SEPTEMBER

The final French advance and the Russian retreat.

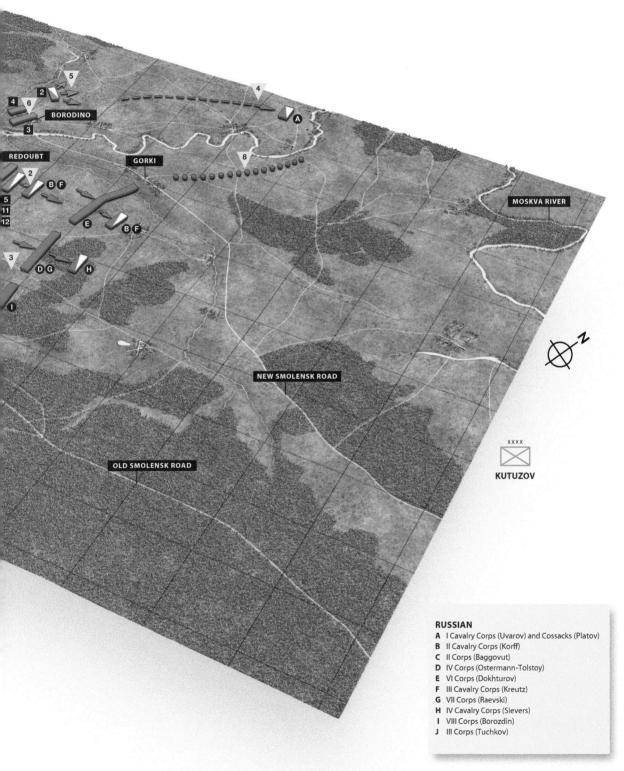

BORODINO

REDOUBT

GORKI

MOSKVA RIVER

NEW SMOLENSK ROAD

OLD SMOLENSK ROAD

KUTUZOV

RUSSIAN
A I Cavalry Corps (Uvarov) and Cossacks (Platov)
B II Cavalry Corps (Korff)
C II Corps (Baggovut)
D IV Corps (Ostermann-Tolstoy)
E VI Corps (Dokhturov)
F III Cavalry Corps (Kreutz)
G VII Corps (Raevski)
H IV Cavalry Corps (Sievers)
I VIII Corps (Borozdin)
J III Corps (Tuchkov)

The field of Borodino: a dreadful spectacle drawn from life by the Württemberg officer Christian Faber du Faur.

field found that 'never did one present so horrible an appearance... soldiers roaming about in all directions, and hunting for provisions.... Round the eagles were seen the remaining officers and subalterns, and a few soldiers, scarcely enough to protect the colours... blackened with powder, and spotted with blood; and yet, in the midst of their rags, their misery, and disasters, they had a proud look, and at the sight of the emperor, uttered some shouts of triumph, but they were rare and excited; for in this army, capable at once of analysis and enthusiasm, every one was sensible of the position.

Napoleon's loss is difficult to establish, estimates ranging from 58,000 to at least 30,000, the latter probably fairly accurate. Ségur remarked that the Russian fieldworks were so carpeted with French dead 'that they appeared to belong more to them than to those who remained standing. There seemed to be more victors killed there, than there were still living.' Some officers wondered at Napoleon's tactics: 'it was a battle without a plan, a mere victory of soldiers, rather than of a general'. They were also astonished at the determination of the enemy: barely 800 had allowed themselves to be taken prisoner, and even 'the dead bodies were rather a proof of the courage of the vanquished, than the evidence of a victory. If the rest retreated in such good order, proud, and so little discouraged, what signified the gain of a field of battle?'

17. Wilson's account of the terrain is in *Narrative*, pp. 134–36.
18. Clausewitz, p. 150.
19. Labaume, E., *A Circumstantial Narrative of the Campaign in Russia*, London, 1814, p. 126.
20. ibid., p. 127.
21. Ségur, Vol. I pp. 320–21.
22. Wilson, *Narrative*, p. 139.
23. Labaume, pp. 131–32.
24. Rapp, J., *Memoirs of General Count Rapp, First Aide-de-Camp to Napoleon*, London 1823, p. 208.
25. Clausewitz, pp. 140–41.
26. Ségur, Vol. I p. 337.
27. Ségur, Vol. I p. 349.
28. Labaume, p. 139.
29. Gourgaud, G., *Napoleon and the Grand Army in Russia, or a Critical Examination of the Work of Count Ph. de Ségur*, London, 1825, p. 212.

THE END OF THE CAMPAIGN

THE MARCH TO MOSCOW

Despite the slaughter, Borodino was not the decisive action that Napoleon so desired. It may be seen as one turning point in the campaign, but it was not conclusive in itself; what followed was less of an inevitable consequence as the result of decisions taken after the fighting abated, although the battle was the most crucial factor in determining those decisions. Borodino was an important step towards Napoleon's destruction; yet at its conclusion Napoleon's army was in a much better state than was Kutuzov's. Some elements of Napoleon's army had not fired a shot, others had been relatively

The vanguard of the Grande Armée sights Moscow. (Print after Alfred Paris)

lightly engaged, whereas Kutuzov had had to call upon the whole of his army, and even then had been forced to cede ground. Napoleon's artillery had swept the field, while Kutuzov's had not been deployed to maximum effect, due in part to Kutaisov's reckless self-sacrifice that deprived the artillery of its leadership, negating the Russian advantage in their preponderance of heavier pieces. In terms of courage and determination the Russian army had performed astonishingly, but at the highest level the leadership was not impressive. Kutuzov was largely absent from the thick of the action, and while Barclay did distinguish himself, Bagration's injury caused some direction of the battle to fall into less capable hands. The initial Russian deployment was poor, unnecessarily exposing some units to enemy fire, while the strength of the right, at the expense of the left, could have been more costly than it proved. In part this necessitated the commitment of the reserve earlier in the action than Barclay had intended, depriving the Russians of the opportunity of a strong counterstroke later in the day. In those that were mounted, the Russian cavalry was considerably distinguished, and for all its apparent failure the flanking movement of Uvarov and Platov was actually very significant.

General Feodor Vassilievich Rostopchin (1763–1826), governor of Moscow, who issued vehement calls to arms and who many held responsible for the deliberate burning of the city. (Engraving by F. Mayer after Gebauer)

On Napoleon's side, his artillery had played a crucial role, and his infantry had attacked with spirit. The handling of the cavalry was less impressive; the nature of the terrain acted against free-flowing manoeuvre, and for too long large bodies of horsemen stood exposed to artillery fire, and the attack of earthworks was not an ideal mode of employment of their real abilities. The Duke of Wellington once remarked that Napoleon tended to use his cuirassiers as 'a kind of accelerated infantry, with which, supported by masses of cannon, he was in the habit of seizing important parts in the centre or flanks of his enemy's position', and Borodino might be seen as an example of this; though once through and past the earthworks the cavalry was vulnerable to Russian countercharges. In tactical terms, the French subordinate commanders had little opportunity for initiative, Napoleon's plans having condemned his army to a succession of frontal assaults on prepared positions. Napoleon's own contribution was limited; he appeared lethargic and unwell, a factor remarked upon by a number of those who were close to him.

In his report to the Tsar, written after the fighting subsided, Kutuzov reported that, 'Your Imperial Majesty's troops fought with incredible valour. The batteries passed from the possession of one party to that of the other, and the result was, that the enemy with his superior force, has, in no one part gained an inch of ground. I remained at night master of the field of battle.'[30] This led the Tsar to award Kutuzov a promotion and a grant of 100,000 roubles – each ordinary soldier received five roubles – but the truth was very different. Accepting the inevitable, late on the day of the battle Kutuzov authorized a withdrawal, appointing General Friedrich Korff, leader of II Cavalry Corps, to command the rearguard. It was no precipitate flight; indeed, Barclay briefly reoccupied the Great Redoubt early on 8 September, the ruined position having been vacated by the Grande Armée after its capture. By mid-morning on 8 September the Russian columns were marching eastwards, towards Mozhaisk, with no immediate pursuit due to the disorganization and exhaustion of Napoleon's army; as Ségur noted, 'The army remained motionless until noon, or rather it might be said there was no longer an army, but a single vanguard. The rest of the troops were dispersed over the field of battle to carry off the wounded.'[31] In the afternoon Murat and part of his cavalry began the pursuit, and on 9 September hurried the Russian rearguard out of Mozhaisk, only to be stopped by a counterattack.

Kutuzov had to decide whether to make another stand or allow Napoleon to occupy Moscow. On 13 September he held a council of war, at which Bennigsen and others were for fighting, but other commanders supported the decision to retreat, for 'the contest was for the Russian empire, and not for the preservation of any particular city or the capital itself'. By abandoning Moscow, the Russian army could retire to regroup and receive reinforcements, while every step eastwards would lengthen Napoleon's line of communications. Similarly, Napoleon had to decide on following the Russian army or retiring to reorganize and renew the war in the spring. Having already marched so far, he remained convinced that the Tsar would be forced to accept his terms; so decided to march towards Moscow. It, and those that followed, were fatal decisions.

At this stage of the campaign, Napoleon had about 95,000 men available for the advance on Moscow. Other elements of the Grande Armée were fully committed to the protection of his flanks: to the north, Gouvion Saint-Cyr with II and VI Corps around Polotsk, with Macdonald's X Corps covering the area from there to the Baltic, holding off Wittgenstein's Russian I Corps;

to the south, the approaching Chichagov was opposed by Reynier's VII Corps, Schwarzenberg's Austrians and, further east, Dombrowski's Division of Poniatowski's V Corps. This left Napoleon with the Imperial Guard, the cavalry, and I, III, IV and the rest of V Corps for his main advance; Junot's VIII Corps was left behind to clear the battlefield of Borodino. Victor's IX Corps was coming up as a reinforcement; he arrived at Smolensk on 27 September.

MOSCOW

On the morning of 14 September Napoleon's vanguard came in sight of Moscow, where a huge evacuation was proceeding; Wilson estimated that 180,000 of the 200,000 inhabitants, with 65,000 vehicles, quit the city and marched eastwards. Murat arrived at Moscow's western gate while this was still in progress, but with insufficient forces to launch a major attack he acceded to a request from General Mikhail Miloradovich, who was supervising the evacuation, for a truce until evening. Napoleon arrived in mid-afternoon; Labaume assessed that the capture of Moscow, the ancient capital regarded by the Russians as almost sacred, 'was one of the most extraordinary occurrences in modern history'[32]. It was not, however, quite the triumph it seemed: for on that very evening a fire broke out that burned unchecked until 20 September, destroying three-quarters of the city. The origin of the conflagration was debated: some thought it accidental, but Russians were reported as having been caught in the act of arson, and it was believed that the city's governor, Feodor Rostopchin, had ordered its destruction. He had issued vehement calls to arms, and deliberately burned his own country house a short distance away as part

The burning of Moscow: suspected arsonists are brought before Napoleon.

of a calculated 'scorched earth' policy to deny resources to the invaders, and had removed the fire-fighting appliances from the city upon its evacuation. He left the invaders a notice affixed to his own burned mansion, recorded by Wilson: 'I voluntarily set the house on fire, that it might not be polluted by your presence… you will find only ashes.'[33] Whatever its cause, the burning of Moscow was seen as visible proof of the Russian determination to continue the resistance; as was Murat's welcome to the city, when some of the remaining inhabitants rushed at him in a fury, one of his officers being dragged from his horse and bitten in the neck until the frenzied Russian was beaten off.

Despite the destruction, enough remained of Moscow to provide quarters for Napoleon's army; ironically, had more been destroyed he might well not have remained in Moscow so long. That he did so was because he believed that the Tsar would have to negotiate, and as early as 20 September he sent a message to the Russians in pursuit of a settlement; he received no reply. While awaiting a response the Grande Armée remained inactive, no serious attempt being made to push further eastwards. The Tsar, however, had no intention of negotiating, and used the respite to reorganize and rearm.

Kutuzov at first moved his forces some 40km (25 miles) south of Moscow, behind the line of the river Pakhra, but when Napoleon's cavalry reconnoitered the area the Russians pulled back a further 50km (30 miles) to the south-west, behind the river Nara, to Tarutino. It was a well-chosen location, facilitating contact with Russian forces marching up from the south, blocking Napoleon's access to the fertile areas south of Moscow, preventing him from sweeping up provisions, and was between the invaders and the great iron-working and arms-manufacturing centre of Tula, from where Kutuzov could draw munitions. While Napoleon remained inactive, the Russian forces were built up to as many as 120,000, and their reorganization included the merger of the two West Armies into one body under Kutuzov. Bagration died of his Borodino injury on 24 September and Barclay retired, ostensibly on grounds of ill-health, though probably he felt that he had been eased from office as a consequence of his continuing unpopularity. The Tsar retired to St Petersburg and from there his advisors developed a plan to assail Napoleon from three sides. In addition to Kutuzov's main army, the Army of the Danube, headed by Admiral Pavel Chichagov, was marching from the south to threaten Napoleon's right rear, while from the north General Ludwig Wittgenstein's army, reinforced by General Steingell (or 'Steinheil') with some 13,000 men from Finland, faced the two corps protecting Napoleon's left flank. In addition, the flanks and communications of the Grande Armée were harassed increasingly by flying columns of Russian cavalry and notably Cossacks, aided by the newly formed *opolchenie* and bands of guerrillas who fell upon Napoleon's foragers, intercepted couriers and cut communications.

As his situation deteriorated, Napoleon remained convinced that the Tsar had to negotiate, and on 5 October sent General Jacques-Alexandre Lauriston, recently his ambassador to Russia, to Kutuzov; Ségur claimed that his final instruction to Lauriston was, 'I want peace, I must have peace, I absolutely will have peace; only save my honour!'[34] When he met Kutuzov Lauriston complained about the barbarity of the Russian marauders and guerrillas, to which Kutuzov replied that the invaders were regarded by the Russians as no better than the horde of Genghis Khan, and that he could only answer for the conduct of the troops in his own army. Kutuzov stated that he had no authority to negotiate, but would convey Napoleon's message to the Tsar; but neither it, nor a further message on 14 October, received any reply.

With seemingly no chance of diplomatic settlement, Napoleon's position became increasingly parlous. To winter in Moscow faced a prospect of starvation; a march against St Petersburg would pit his declining resources against a Russian army increasing in strength; he could move to another region of Russia where supplies might be found, even if it meant fighting his way there; or he could withdraw along his route of advance, already denuded of

Napoleon leaves Moscow at the beginning of the retreat. (Print after Christian Faber du Faur)

supplies. With no reply from the Tsar forthcoming, Napoleon decided to retire upon the depot of Smolensk, but not by the previous route, instead swinging south, towards Kaluga, where supplies would be more plentiful. Before he could commence, however, the Russians attacked Murat's advance post at Vinkovo, south-west of Moscow, on 18 October. They achieved considerable surprise – Sebastiani, commanding II Cavalry Corps after Montbrun's death, was blamed – but the attack was not pressed as hard as it might have been, Kutuzov being unenthusiastic about the plan urged on him by subordinates, and Baggovut was killed. It was, nevertheless, a considerable success that exposed the weakness of Napoleon's cavalry, now losing mounts to fatigue and hunger at an alarming rate, and it forced Napoleon into action. He ordered the evacuation of Moscow a day before he had originally intended, and on the morning of 19 October he left the city at the head of his army.

THE RETREAT

At this stage Napoleon's army was still about 95,000 strong, but it was accompanied by a vast number of camp-followers and perhaps as many as 40,000 wheeled vehicles; army and followers were loaded with loot so that Ségur compared them to 'a horde of Tartars after a successful invasion'. Such an enormous body could only hinder the manoeuvres of the army and consume rations and fodder needed for the combatants; and whereas the Russian forces were increasing steadily in number, Napoleon had few reserves upon which to call, beyond Victor's IX Corps.

Even before Napoleon began his retreat from Moscow, the Russian pincer had begun to move. The force guarding Napoleon's left, II and VI Corps led by Gouvion Saint-Cyr, was engaged by Wittgenstein at Polotsk (18–20 October) and was forced to begin a withdrawal south-westwards. Saint-Cyr had to relinquish command after being shot in the foot; Oudinot, who had been recuperating from a wound sustained in August returned to command his own II Corps and Saint-Cyr's VI Corps as well. To the south of Napoleon's intended line of retreat, Schwarzenberg's Austrians and Reynier's VII Corps were held in check by the Russians and were unable to prevent the northward march of Chichagov's army.

On leaving Moscow, Napoleon intended to slip around Kutuzov's left flank and make a wide sweep to approach Smolensk from the south, over territory not already stripped of supplies and fodder; but Kutuzov, believing Napoleon's approach to be merely a strong foraging party, sent Dokhturov with his VI Corps, and cavalry, to intercept. On 24 October they clashed with Napoleon's vanguard, Eugène's IV Corps, at Maloyaroslavets; the fight was fierce and although the Russians fell back, Napoleon realized that to continue would have meant further heavy combat. Then, on the following day, while reconnoitring Napoleon and his staff were attacked by Cossacks who emerged unexpectedly from the morning mist; the emperor's escort had a sharp fight until reinforcements arrived, and Napoleon was hustled away to safety. It was one of the closest escapes he ever had, and whether it had any profound effect upon him is uncertain, but he held a council of war in which conflicting opinions were aired. Murat, characteristically, was for fighting their way through; but others, aware of the army's declining strength, were against. Napoleon agreed: the army would withdraw and resume its westward march to Smolensk over the route they had come, with all that entailed concerning the shortage of supplies. On 29 October they recrossed the battlefield of Borodino, an unnerving sight even to the strongest, the terrain still littered with unburied bodies, half-eaten by dogs and birds of prey.

Ironically, Kutuzov had not been prepared for another major battle and was himself beginning to withdraw when Napoleon's intentions became obvious. Kutuzov realized that another great battle was unnecessary, and that privations and fatigue could destroy the invaders, so he limited his strategy to a not very close pursuit plus the harassment of Cossacks, cavalry and guerrillas, with some more serious forays against the retiring invaders. These were possible because of the huge extent of Napoleon's column of retreat, some 80km (50 miles) from front to rear, and on 3 November the rearguard, Davout's I Corps, was almost overwhelmed near Vyazma by General Mikhail

ABOVE
Ney on the retreat, where his conduct confirmed his nickname 'bravest of the brave'. (Print after Langlois)

BELOW
During the retreat, Russian civilians are brought to Napoleon (centre) for interrogation; Murat is second from right, in the plumed hat. (Print after Verestchagin)

Napoleon and his escort
is surprised by Cossacks,
25 October 1812. (Print after
Chelminski)

Miloradovich with the Russian II and IV Corps. Davout was dragged free by Eugène, his command in disorder, and Ney with III Corps took over rearguard duties.

Napoleon's situation was beginning to deteriorate alarmingly as discipline began to collapse and parts of the army turned into a mass of fugitives around a nucleus of stalwarts who continued to maintain their order. With Victor having to deploy much of his command to support Oudinot against Wittgenstein's pressure, Napoleon had little chance of receiving support. To ease pressure on supplies, he ordered Eugène north towards the base at Vitebsk, but he was turned back by Platov and his Cossacks. On 9 November Napoleon reached Smolensk to find its supply depot emptied by the administrative units that were leading the retreat; any hope of wintering there was gone, and the retreat would have to continue. On the same day there was a severe frost, followed by heavy snow and bitter temperatures that compounded the army's misery, turning what was already a severe trial into an ordeal of unimaginable proportions. The cavalry was almost extinct and the few surviving horses, and officers no longer with commands, were formed into the so-called 'sacred squadrons' to provide at least a semblance of a mounted arm. Baggage and guns had to be abandoned as their horses died, and General Jean Rapp summed up their plight: 'The cold, the privations, were extreme; the hour of disasters had come on us!... At every step we were obliged to halt, and fight.... Cold, hunger, the Cossacks – every scourge was let loose upon us. The army was sinking under the weight of its misfortunes; the road was strewed with the dead: our sufferings exceeded imagination'[35.]

The Grande Armée stumbled westwards, in Labaume's words 'scarcely able to drag themselves along... nothing to eat, nothing to drink, shivering with cold, and groaning with pain.... The soldier no longer obeyed his officer, the officer separated himself from his general. The regiments disbanded... searching for food, they spread themselves over the plain, burning and destroying whatever fell in their way'[36] In addition to the

The Retreat

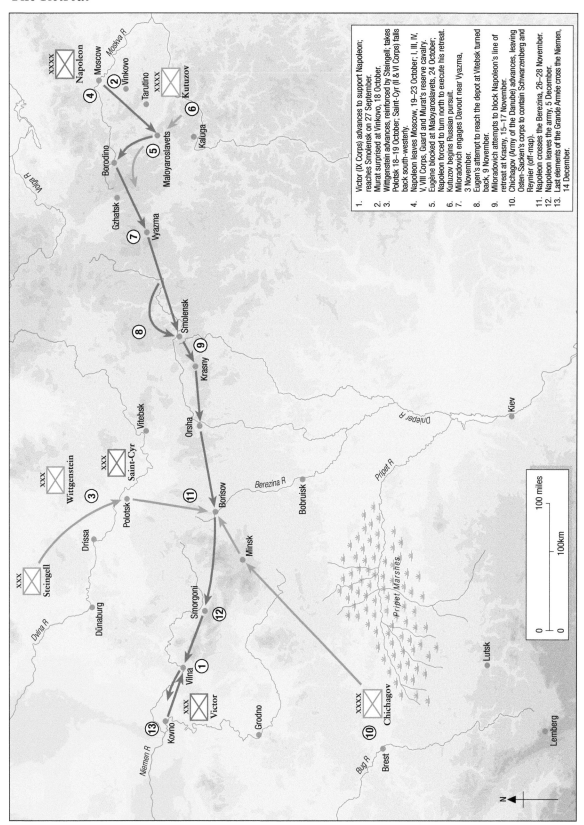

1. Victor (IX Corps) advances to support Napoleon; reaches Smolensk on 27 September.
2. Murat surprised at Vinkovo, 18 October.
3. Wittgenstein advances, reinforced by Steingell; takes Polotsk 18–19 October; Saint-Cyr (II & VI Corps) falls back south-westerly.
4. Napoleon leaves Moscow, 19–23 October; I, III, IV, V, VIII Corps, Guard and Murat's reserve cavalry.
5. Eugène blocked at Maloyaroslavets, 24 October; Napoleon forced to turn north to execute his retreat.
6. Kutuzov begins Russian pursuit.
7. Miloradovich engages Davout near Vyazma, 3 November.
8. Eugen's attempt to reach the depot at Vitebsk turned back, 9 November.
9. Miloradovich attempts to block Napoleon's line of retreat at Krasny, 15–17 November.
10. Chichagov (Army of the Danube) advances, leaving Osten-Sacken's corps to contain Schwarzenberg and Reynier (off-map).
11. Napoleon crosses the Berezina, 26–28 November.
12. Napoleon leaves the army, 5 December.
13. Last elements of the Grande Armée cross the Niemen, 14 December.

Marshal Nicolas-Charles Oudinot, duc de Reggio (1767–1847), leader of II Corps. Probably the most frequently wounded senior commander of the period, he was hit by a grapeshot at Polotsk and temporarily turned over his command to Saint-Cyr, but returned to play an important role at the Berezina, where he was wounded again. (Print by Wolf after Lefevre)

ever-hovering Cossacks, Miloradovich cut the road near Krasny after Napoleon and the Guard had passed, and after Eugène and what remained of his corps broke through, on 17 November Napoleon had to turn back to rescue the remainder, counterattacking with the Imperial Guard and pushing aside the Russian roadblock.

The army crossed the Dnieper at Orsha unopposed, though Ségur calculated that its combatant part now numbered no more than 6,000 men of the Guard, 4,000 of I Corps and 1,800 of IV Corps, the remainder virtually extinguished as cohesive units. Ney was believed lost; but on 21 November he and the survivors of his corps rejoined the army, to Napoleon's unconcealed delight. It was at this point, for his conduct of the rearguard, that Napoleon bestowed upon Ney the entirely deserved sobriquet 'bravest of the brave'.

THE BEREZINA

One further hurdle remained: the river Berezina, with its main crossing point at Borisov. A guard had been placed there, reinforced by Dombrowski, but on 22 November news reached the army that it had been lost, attacked by the vanguard of Admiral Chichagov's army, which had already taken the store-depot of Minsk. Napoleon's route of escape was blocked. Realizing its significance, Oudinot counterattacked and regained the town, but the Russians burned the bridge before it could be secured.

Napoleon always claimed to place great faith in luck, and now it came to his aid. As VI Corps had been sent westwards under its new commander, the Bavarian General Carl Philipp Wrede, it had been accompanied by General Jean-Baptiste Corbineau's brigade of Oudinot's corps cavalry. Anxious to rejoin his proper command, Corbineau marched south-east to the Berezina, intending to cross at Borisov, until he learned that the Russians had seized the crossing. One of his regiments, being Polish in composition, was able to converse with the local inhabitants and discovered a ford at Studianka, about 12km (7 miles) north of Borisov. Corbineau used it to rejoin Oudinot, and when he learned of the ford Napoleon determined to cross the river there, rather than have to march north and fight Wittgenstein. He ordered Oudinot to demonstrate south of Borisov, on the east bank of the river, to deceive Chichagov into thinking that there was a ford there; the ploy worked, the Russians moved to counter this imaginary threat, and the line of the river from Borisov to Studianka was left virtually undefended.

The weather, however, had turned against Napoleon. It is often thought that it was snow and freezing temperatures that destroyed the Grande Armée, but it was rising temperatures that proved the greatest obstacle: the Berezina was not so frozen as to be crossed on foot, and the accumulating flood-waters caused the river to swell to a width of about 200m (650ft). At Orsha the army's pontoon-train had been burned to prevent its capture, its surviving horses used to pull artillery; but the commander of the pontoon-train, General Jean-Baptiste Eblé, had preserved enough tools and iron fittings to construct two improvised bridges over the Berezina, initiative that saved what remained of the army. The efforts of his pontooneers were truly heroic, the equal of any deed performed during the campaign: labouring in freezing water and repairing frequent collapses, they kept open the path of retreat. II Corps crossed the river first, securing the west bank, and it was followed by the cohesive part of Napoleon's army, Victor and IX Corps remaining on the east bank as a rearguard against Wittgenstein.

On 27 November Chichagov, having realized his error, marched north along the west bank of the Berezina and began to attack Oudinot; and, having restored the Borisov bridge and having established contact with Wittgenstein, the two launched a concerted attack on the following day against Oudinot and the remains of Ney's III Corps on the west bank, and against Victor on the east. Oudinot was wounded again and Ney took command, stabilizing the position by counterattacks. Wittgenstein's attack on the east bank was even more desperate, the vast horde of stragglers and followers from Napoleon's army rushing towards the bridges, countless being trampled in the stampede

RETREAT FROM MOSCOW (pp. 84–85)

As exemplified in this illustration, the unimaginable horrors of the retreat arose from a combination of fatigue, extreme cold, hunger and the constant danger of marauding Cossacks who tracked the weary columns, ready to isolate and over-run stragglers or small bodies, engendering fear and anxiety. Raymond de Fezensac, commander of the French 4th Line, described how the cold weather 'put the finishing stroke to the sufferings of men already half dead with hunger and fatigue' amid, 'boundless plains covered with snow, endless forests, [a] countless column… staggering at every step, and sinking beneath the carcases of horses and the lifeless bodies of their companions in misery'. Each night's halt, he wrote, resembled a field of battle, from the number who had lain to sleep and never wakened. The bodies of the dead were stripped of clothing to provide additional insulation for the living, and every morsel of food was devoured as self-preservation eclipsed humanity. The fact that the army included countless followers, women and children, only compounded the horror. Even so, Fezensac described his own regiment as a 'community in misfortune', and recounted that no officer or soldier who came into possession of a scrap of bread ever failed to share it with him, their colonel. (Fezensac pp. 148–51). In this illustration a column of French infantry **(1)**, accompanied by cavalrymen who have lost their horses **(2)**, and by wives and children **(3)**, trudge past wrecked transports and the bodies of those already fallen. Cossacks hover on the skyline **(4)**.

Driving off Cossacks: in the earlier stages of the retreat some artillery pieces were retained by the wreck of the Grande Armée until the draught horses were lost. (Print after Christian Faber du Faur)

or drowning when pushed into the river. Victor's men fought furiously to hold their position, the Baden Hussars and Hessian Chevauxlegers helping to hold back the enemy by their famous 'charge of death' from which few returned. Russian pressure slackened after this exploit and in the evening Victor began to withdraw across the river. By early morning on 29 November the last combatant elements of the Grande Armée were across the Berezina. Eblé was ordered to destroy the bridges to hinder Russian pursuit, but he delayed for some three hours to permit more of the stragglers to escape. At about 8.30am he set fire to the bridges, marooning thousands on the east bank; many made a last attempt to cross the burning bridges to safety or threw themselves into the freezing water, and countless souls perished in the attempt. The scene was unimaginable and apocalyptic, and the fact that any escaped at all was due to the heroic efforts of the troops who battled to keep the Russians back, and to Eblé and his band of determined pontooneers. Worn out by his exertions, Eblé died on 30 December.

At the Berezina, members of IX Corps, still under arms (right) confront the mass of fugitives after all order and discipline was lost. The men in the centre are melting snow for drinking water. (Print after Christian Faber du Faur)

The Berezina

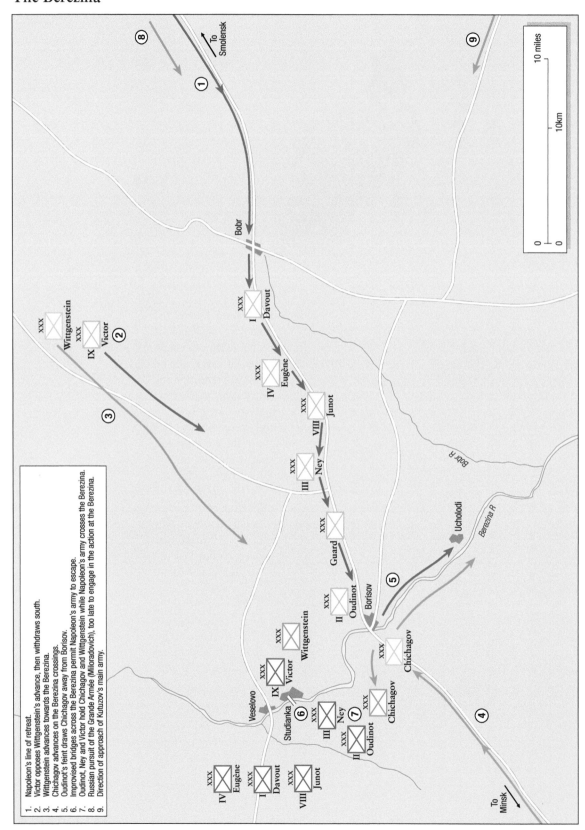

1. Napoleon's line of retreat.
2. Victor opposes Wittgenstein's advance, then withdraws south.
3. Wittgenstein advances towards the Berezina.
4. Chichagov advances on the Berezina crossings.
5. Oudinot's feint draws Chichagov away from Borisov.
6. Improvised bridges across the Berezina permit Napoleon's army to escape.
7. Oudinot, Ney and Victor hold Chichagov and Wittgenstein while Napoleon's army crosses the Berezina.
8. Russian pursuit of the Grande Armée (Miloradovich), too late to engage in the action at the Berezina.
9. Direction of approach of Kutuzov's main army.

Crossing the Berezina: a cuirassier leads his family to safety. (Print after Charlet)

The retreat staggered onwards, continually harassed by Cossacks and the vanguard of the pursuing Russian forces, but there was no need for the Russians to initiate any major action, for fatigue, cold, hunger and demoralization destroyed what remained of Napoleon's army. On 2 December it was reported that only some 9,000 to 13,000 troops were still effective, of whom some 2,000 were in the rearguard, led by Ney. Every step westwards was marked by the death of men, women and children too exhausted to carry on. On 5 December at Smorgoni Napoleon left the army, entrusting it to Murat's care, to return to Paris to organize a new army for the campaign of the coming year. He was criticized by some for abandoning those who had followed him to Moscow and back, but in effect the army no longer existed, and his continuing presence with what remained could have achieved little. On 11–12 December the troops crawled into Kovno, with its crossing over the Niemen; it was said that the last member of the Grande Armée to leave Russia under arms was Ney himself. He was unrecognized by an acquaintance shortly after, so changed was he in appearance by the ordeal; he declared that 'I am the rearguard of the Grande Armée!' and that he had fired the last shot over the bridge at Kovno. He, at least, was defiant to the last.

Raymond de Fezensac, who had taken command of the French 4th Line following the death of its colonel at Borodino, contrasted his departure from Paris and his return at the end of the campaign: 'I arrived alone in the night, on a dung-cart, wrapped in a wolf's skin, at the same house which, nine months previously, I had quitted amidst such immense preparations, and with so many brilliant hopes of success and glory.'[37] It was an appropriate analogy for the whole campaign.

30. Translation from *The Anti-Gallican Monitor*, 11 October 1812.
31. Ségur, Vol. I p. 355.
32. Labaume, p. 210.
33. Wilson, *Narrative*, p. 180.
34. Ségur, Vol. II p. 71.
35. Rapp, pp. 230–31.
36. Labaume, pp. 282–83.
37. Fezensac, R., *A Journal of the Russian Campaign of 1812*, London, 1852, p. 181.

AFTERMATH

Losses in the expedition to Russia are difficult to estimate, but Napoleon probably lost about 370,000 men dead and 200,000 captured, of whom at least half would not survive; he also lost about 1,000 cannon. This was not the only gauge of his disaster, for its morale effects were at least as profound as allies began to desert him. The Prussian element of Macdonald's X Corps, which had held Napoleon's left flank, had always been the most unwilling of allies, and in response to Russian overtures declared themselves neutral by the Convention of Tauroggen on 30 December. A month later the Austrians who had held the extreme right flank followed suit, precursors of both states joining Russia in the continuing fight against Napoleon in 1813. News of Napoleon's catastrophe in Russia emboldened all his opponents, removing his aura of invincibility, from the continuing war in Spain to the burgeoning 'liberation' movement in Germany. Fears of Napoleon's prowess were even replaced by ridicule, as in a rhyme published in the British newspaper the *Northampton Mercury*, which printed 'Bonaparte's Last Bulletin from Russia': 'The Cossacks

Napoleon leaves the Grande Armée at Smorgoni on 5 December 1812 to return to Paris. (Print after J. Rosen)

slain, the Kremlin burnt,/The Country spoil'd! Enough./Back we began to march; but O!/That fellow Kut-us-off.'[38]

Russian losses in the campaign were probably about 150,000 dead and countless wounded, but the ultimate victor did not survive to see the end of Napoleon's empire that had begun to fall in Russia. Kutuzov was promoted to field marshal and was given the title Prince of Smolensk, but remained unpopular with some in the highest authority, was relieved of his command and died on 28 April 1813.

Napoleon bore ultimate responsibility for the 1812 campaign and its consequences, from its initiation to operational decisions and for delaying so long in Moscow that it was inevitable that his withdrawal would fall victim to the climate. Despite the resources available to him, the task had been too great from the outset, given the determination exhibited by every level of Russian society. In later life Napoleon acknowledged the power of an enemy possessed of geographical advantages and an immense population, 'brave, hardy, devoted and passive, including those numerous uncivilized hordes, to whom privations and wandering are the natural state of existence', with an army which, if victorious, could overwhelm everything in its path, or if defeated, 'retiring amidst the cold and desolation, that may be called its reserves in case of defeat. Is not this the head of the Hydra, the Antaeus of fable, which can only be subdued by grasping it bodily… but where is the Hercules to be found? France alone could think of such an achievement, and it must be confessed we made but an awkward attempt at it.'[39] Ségur concurred: 'The genius of Napoleon, in attempting to soar above time, climate, and distances, had, as it were, lost itself in space: great as was its measure, it had been beyond it.'[40] Despite the errors that preceded and followed it, a pivotal factor of the campaign, and perhaps of the fate of his entire empire, had been Napoleon's failure to annihilate the Russian army at Borodino; and the determination of the gallant Russians who had defended their homeland to the last extremity.

38. *Northampton Mercury*, 12 December 1812.
39. Las Cases, Vol. IV p. 74.
40. Ségur, Vol. II p. 180.

THE BATTLEFIELD TODAY

The significance of Borodino and its battlefield in the Russian national consciousness was exemplified by a plea made by Kutuzov in the month following the battle. He urged that the field, and its fortifications, be left unmolested for posterity; to be allowed to suffer the natural process of decay, but not to be changed by the improvements of agriculture. Although not unchanged from its appearance in 1812, Borodino has suffered less than some battlefields and has become almost a shrine to the determination and bravery of the Russian army that fought there.

The stark terrain shown in some contemporary illustrations, and in places described by some combatants, has taken on a more verdant aspect over two centuries, including the continuance of the presence of some woodland as existed in 1812; and while some of the original evidences of mankind have disappeared, others have replaced them. The most significant feature of the field, roughly in its centre, the Great or Raevski Redoubt, apparently disappeared in a relatively short period after the battle: it was constructed hastily and was severely damaged during the fighting. Its tactical significance, however, may still be appreciated from the site, in the field of fire it provided against troops attacking from Napoleon's position; and as the pivotal position in the battle, it is appropriate that the main monument to the Russian army is sited there. Another generation of small fortifications were constructed nearby during World War II.

The *flèches* no doubt suffered the same fate as the Great Redoubt, but for the centenary of the battle they were reconstructed, probably rather more elaborately than the hastily raised earthworks of 1812. The nearby monastery was constructed subsequent to the battle. The principal watercourses that exerted some influence on the events of the battle are still evident, as is Borodino village, the church with its two domes still extant, marking the largely unchanged nature of the field. The site of the Shevardino Redoubt was also reconstructed for the centenary, and appropriately it is there that the main monument to the Grande Armée is sited, topped by an eagle, marking the position of Napoleon's headquarters during the battle. Similarly, other monuments near Gorki mark the evident location of Kutuzov's personal position.

Among the most obvious features of the battlefield is the proliferation of monuments, which range from the commemoration of individuals and Russian units that fought there, to the location of artillery positions, both Russian and French. The former include monuments commemorating corps and divisions and some for particular regiments, ranging from the Lifeguard to the *opolchenie*, some detailing the casualties incurred by the units involved.

Very few of those who fell at Borodino have any individual, marked resting place, and perhaps the two most notable monuments are to commanders who did not actually die at Borodino. Bagration, mortally wounded there but who died subsequently, lies near the battlefield's main monument, at the site of the Great Redoubt. General Dmitri Neverovski, who was killed at Leipzig some 13 months after Borodino, is interred in the proximity of the *flèches*, near to the monument to his gallant 27th Division, in the position they defended so stoutly. The field also includes a monument to the descendents of those who fought at Borodino, the Red Army of World War II.

West of the Great Redoubt is the impressive battlefield museum, though one of the largest commemorations of the battle was established in Moscow: the panorama. This huge artwork, part painting and part diorama, some 115 by 15m (380 by 50ft) in magnitude, was commissioned to mark the centenary of the battle from the artist Franz Roubaud, who had previously created a similar panorama depicting the siege of Sebastopol to mark the 50th anniversary of that event in 1905. The original rotunda that housed the panorama was closed in 1918 but the painting was restored in 1946 and 1962, and a new rotunda was built in Moscow for the 150th anniversary of the battle.

BIBLIOGRAPHY

(Details are given of English-language editions.)

Adam, A., *Napoleon's Army in Russia: The Illustrated Memoirs of Albrecht Adam*, trans. J. North, Barnsley, 2005

Bourgogne, A. J. B. F., *The Memoirs of Sergeant Bourgogne 1812–1813*, trans. & ed. P. Cottin and M. Henault, London, 1899

Brett-James, A., *1812: Eyewitness Accounts of Napoleon's Defeat in Russia*, London, 1966

Britten Austin, P., *1812: The March on Moscow*, London, 1993

——, *1812: Napoleon in Moscow*, London, 1995

——, *1812: The Great Retreat*, London, 1996

Caulaincourt, A. de, *With Napoleon in Russia: The Memoirs of General de Caulaincourt, Duke of Vicenza*, ed. J. Hanoteau, intro. G. Libaire, New York, 1935

Chandler, D., *The Campaigns of Napoleon*, London, 1967

Clausewitz, C. M. von, *The Campaign of 1812 in Russia*, London, 1843

Chuquet, A., *Human Voices from the Russian Campaign of 1812*, London, 1913

Duffy, C., *Borodino and the War of 1812*, London, 1972

Esposito, V. J., and Elting, R., *Military History and Atlas of the Napoleonic Wars*, London, 1964

Faber du Faur, C. W., *With Napoleon in Russia: The Illustrated Memoirs of Faber du Faur*, 1812, ed. & trans. J. North, London, 2001

Fezensac, R., *A Journal of the Russian Campaign of 1812*, intro. W. Knollys, London, 1852

Gourgaud, G., *Napoleon and the Grand Army in Russia, or a Critical Examination of the Work of Count Ph. de Ségur*, London, 1825

Hourtoulle, F. G., *Borodino – the Moskova: The Battle for the Redoubts*, trans. A. McKay, Paris, 2000

Josselson, M., & Josselson, D., *The Commander: A Life of Barclay de Tolly*, Oxford, 1980

Labaume, E., *A Circumstantial Narrative of the Campaign in Russia*, London, 1814

Nafziger, G. F., *Napoleon's Invasion of Russia*, Novato, CA, 1988

Olivier, D., *The Burning of Moscow*, London, 1964

Palmer, A., *Napoleon in Russia*, London, 1967

——, *Russia in War and Peace*, London, 1972

Roeder, H., *The Ordeal of Campaign Roeder*, trans. & ed. H. Roeder, London, 1960

Ségur, P. de, *History of the Expedition to Russia undertaken by the Emperor Napoleon in the Year 1812*, London, 1825

Smith, D., *Borodino*, Morton-in-Marsh, 1998

Vossler, H. A., *With Napoleon in Russia 1812*, trans. W. Wallich, London, 1969.

Wilson, Sir Robert, *Narrative of Events during the Invasion of Russia by Napoleon Bonaparte*, ed. Revd. H. Randolph, London, 1860

——, *General Wilson's Journal 1812–14*, ed. A. Brett-James, London, 1964

INDEX

Note: Locators in **bold** refer to
photographs, plates and diagrams

Alexander I, Tsar of Russia 5–6, **6**
  and the Battle of Borodin (1812) 74
  his plans 19–23
  the invasion 29, 31, 36–39
  on Kutuzov 37
  refusal to negotiate 75, 76
artillery
  French 46, 47–48, 61, 73, 74
  Russian 43, 53, **68**, 73
Augereau, Marshal Pierre-Francois 19
Austria 5, 6

Baggovut, General Karl 41, 43, 53, 57,
  65, 78
Bagration, General of Infantry Peter
  Ivanovich (1765–1812) **12**, 13, 22, 27,
  29, 30, 31, 33, 41, 44, 53, 57, 76, 93
'Bagration *flèches*' 41, 92
Barclay de Tolly, General of Infantry
  Mikhail Andreas (1761–1818) **12**,
  12–13, 21–22, 27, 29, 30, 31, 32, 33,
  36, 38, 41, 48, 53, 57, 64, 69, 73, 76
Beauharnais, Eugène de, Viceroy of Italy
  (1781–1824) **9**, 10, 17, 27, 30, **31**,
  35, 39, 45, 46, 48, 53, 56, 63, 64,
  79, 80
Belliard, General Auguste 36, 61
Bennigsen, Levin 38, 39, 45, 48, 74
Berezina river 82–89
Bernadotte, Jean-Baptiste 5, 6
Berthier, Marshal Louis-Alexandre,
  prince de Neuchâtel 19, 69
Bessières, Marshal Jean-Baptiste 17, 63
Bonaparte, Jérôme, King of Westphalia
  (1784–1860) 11, 18, 27, 30–31
Bonaparte, Joseph 5
Bonaparte, Napoleon 5–6
  arrival at the battlefield 43–47
  the battle begins 47–49
  the battle for Smolensk 33–36
  crossing the Berezina 82–89
  and the defeat at Salamanca 46
  the Duke of Wellington on 74
  the end of the battle 65–72
  the Great Redoubt **60**, **62**, 63–64,
    68, **69**
  health 46–47, 74
  his plans 16–19
  the invasion 27–36, 38–39
  the march to Moscow 73–75
  Moscow 75–78, **76**, **77**
  the retreat 78–89, **79**, **80**
  returns to Paris 89, **90**
  and the Russian centre 53–57
  and the Russian left wing 49–53
  and the Russian right wing 61–63

Semenovskaya 57–61
the Shevardino Redoubt 43–45
uniform **5**, **30**
Bonnamy, General Charles-Auguste
  56, 57
Borisov 82
Borodino, Battle of (1812) 40–72
  the battlefield today 92–93
Borozdin, General 41, 43
Borrelli, Adjutant-Commandant
  Charles-Luc 61
Britain 5, 6
Broussier, General Jean-Baptiste 53,
  56, 63
Bucharest, Treaty of (1812) 6

casualties
  French 33, 38, **38**, 44, 63, 72, 90
  Russian 44, 48, 56–57, 64, 69, 91
Caulaincourt, General Armand-Auguste
  de 6, 35–36, 64
Caulaincourt, General Auguste-Jean de
  63, 64, **68**
Chichagov, Admiral Pavel (1767–1849)
  14–15, 22, 75, 77, 78, 82, 83
chronology 7–8
Clausewitz, Carl von 12, 29, 37, 38, 40–
  41, 43, 57, 62, 63, 65, 69
commanders
  French commanders 9–12
  Russian commanders 12–15
Compans, General Jean-Dominique 43,
  44, 45, 48
Constantine, Grand Duke 43, 49
'Continental System,' the 5
Convention of Tauroggen 90
Corbineau, General Jean-Baptiste 82

Davout, Marshal Louis-Nicolas, duc
  d'Auerstädt, prince d'Eckmühl
  (1770–1823) 9–10, **10**, 17, 30, 31,
  33, 35, 39, 44, 45, 48, 57, 79, 80
Dessaix, General Joseph-Marie 48, 49
Dokhturov, General Dmitri 33, 41, 43,
  53, 60, 79
Dombrowski, General 75, 82
Drissa 29, 30, 31
Dufour, General François-Marie 60

Eblé, General Jean-Baptiste 82, 87
Elchingen (1805) 10
Ermolov, General Alexei 56
Essarts, General Francois Ledru des 48

Faur, Christian Faber du 72
Fezensac, Raymond de **86**, 89
fortifications, Battle of Borodin 41
French army
  aftermath of the battle 90–91

arrival at the battlefield 43–47
the battle for Smolensk 33–36
Battle of Borodino (1812) 40–72
casualties 33, 38, **38**, 44, 63, 72, 90
chronology 7–8
commanders 9–12
crossing the Berezina 82–89
the end of the battle 65–72
the Great Redoubt 47–48, 53–57,
  60, **62**, 63–64, **68**, **69**
the invasion 27–39
the march to Moscow 73–75
Moscow 75–78
Orders of Battle 23–26
plans 16–19
the retreat 78–89, **86**
and the Russian centre 53–57
and the Russian left wing 49–53
and the Russian right wing 61–63
Semenovskaya 57–61
the Shevardino Redoubt 43–45
strength and organization of the
  forces 16–19, 39, 46, 74–75
tactics 9–10
uniform **5**, **16**, **17**, **18**, **30**, **68**
weapons **32**, 46, 47–48, 53, 61,
  73, 74
Friant, General Louis 57, 60

Germany 90
Gorchakov, Prince Andrei 43
Gorki 40, 48, 57, 69, 92
Gourgaud, Gaspard 44, 45, 46, 69
Great Redoubt, the 41, 45, 47–48,
  53–57, **60**, **62**, 63–64, **68**, **69**, 92
Grouchy, General Emmanuel
  (1766–1847) 18, 45, 57, **57**, 63, 64
Gzhatsk 39

Inkovo 32

Junot, General Jean-Andoche, duc
  d'Abrantès (1771–1813) **11**, 11–12,
  35, 39, 49, 75

Kamenka stream 40
Kolotcha stream 40, 41, 43, 45, 48,
  53, 62
Konovnitsyn, General Pyotr 49, 53,
  56, 57
Korff, General Friedrich 41, 43, 74
Kovno 29, 89
Krasny 32, 82
Kreutz, General 41, 43, 56
Kutaisov, General Alexander 56–57
Kutuzov, General of Infantry Mikhail
  Larionovich (1745–1813) 13, **14**,
  37–39, 40–43, 45, 46, 48, 49, 53, 57,
  61, 69, 73, 74, 76, 79, 91

Labaume, Eugène 44–45, 46, 75, 80
Langeron, General Louis-Alexandre
    14–15
Latour-Maubourg, General Marie-Victor
    18, 57, 60, 63, **69**
Lauriston, General Jacques-Alexandre 76
Lavrov, General Nikolai 48
Leipzig, Battle of (1813) 11, **11**
Lejeune, Louis **52**
Likachev, General Pyotr 56
Löwenstern, Waldemar von 56
Lubino 35

Macdonald, Marshal Jacques-Etienne,
    duc de Tarente (1765–1840) 19, 27,
    30, 74, **78**, 90
Maloyaroslavets 79
Marbot, Jean-Baptiste de 20, **53**
Mecklenburg, Prince Karl von 44
Miloradovich, General Mikhail
    Andreivich (1770–1825) 15, 38, 43,
    75, 79–80, 82
Minsk 30, 82
Mohilev 30, 31
Montbrun, General Louis-Pierre
    (1770–1812) 17, **53**, 63
Morand, General 56, 64
Moscow 27, 36, 37, 40, 74, **74**, 75–78,
    93
Moskva River 40
Mouton, General Georges 61
Mozhaisk 40, 74
Murat, Marshal Joachim, King of Naples
    (1767–1815) 9, **10**, 17, 30, 31,
    32–33, 35, 39, 43, 49, **49**, **52**, 57,
    60, 61, 63, 69, 74, 75, 76, 78, 79, **79**
muskets 32

Nansouty, General Etienne-Marie 17,
    39, 57, 60
Nara river 76
Neverovski, General Dmitri Petrovich
    (1771–1813) 15, 32–33, 43–44,
    49, 93
Ney, Marshal Michel, duc d'Elchingen
    (1769–1815) 10, **10**, 17, 30, 33, 35,
    39, 45, 47, 48, 53, 61, **79**, 80, 82, 83,
    83, 89

opposing commanders
    French commanders 9–12
    Russian commanders 12–15
Orders of Battle
    French 23–26
    Russian 26
Ornano, General Philippe-Antoine 62
Orsha 82
Ostermann-Tolstoy, General Alexander
    Ivanovich 41, 43, 61
Ostrovno 31, **35**, **37**
Oudinot, Marshal Nicolas-Charles, duc
    de Reggio (1767–1847) 11, 17, 30,
    31–32, 78, 80, 82, **82**, 83

Pahlen, General Peter 41
Pakhra river 76
Phull, Colonel Ernst von 29
Platov, General Matvei Ivanovich
    (1751–1818) 14, **14**, 22, 32, 41,
    56, 61–62, 80
Plauzonne, General Louis-Auguste
    48
Poland 5
Polotsk 31–32, 74, 78, **82**
Poniatowski, Prince Josef (1763–1813)
    10–11, **11**, 18, 33, 39, 44, 45, **47**,
    48, 49, 65
Porter, Robert Ker 13
Prussia 5, 6

Raevski, General Nikolai Nikolaivich
    (1771–1829) 15, 33, 41, 43, 53,
    56, 57
Raevski Redoubt, the see Great Redoubt,
    the
Rapp, General Jean 48, 49, 80
Reynier, General Jean-Louis 18, 32,
    75, 78
Rostopchin, General Feodor Vassilievich
    (1763–1826) 38, **74**, 75–76
Roussel, General Jean-Claude 48
Russian army
    aftermath of the battle 91
    the battle begins 47–49
    the battle for Smolensk 33–36
    Battle of Borodino (1812) 40–72
    the battlefield 40–43
    casualties 44, 48, 56–57, 64,
        69, 91
    the centre during the battle 53–57
    chronology 7–8
    commanders 12–15
    the end of the battle 65–72
    the French arrive at the battlefield
        43–47
    and the French crossing of the
        Berezina 82–89
    and the French invasion 27–39
    and the French march to Moscow
        73–75
    and the French retreat 78–89, **86**
    the Great Redoubt 47–48, 53–57,
        60, **62**, 63–64, 68, 69
    Kutuzov takes command 36–39
    the left wing during the battle
        49–53
    Moscow 75–78
    Orders of Battle 26
    plans 19–23
    the right wing during the battle
        61–63
    Semenovskaya 57–61
    the Shevardino Redoubt 43–45
    strength and organization of the
        forces 19–23, 43, 76
    uniforms 20, **22**, 65
    weapons **21**, 43, 44, 53, **68**, 73

Sablonnière, General Charles-Etienne de
    la 35
Saint-Cyr, General Laurent Gouvion
    (1764–1830) 17, 32, 74, 78, **78**
Schwarzenberg, Prince Karl Philipp 19,
    27, 32, 75, 78
Sebastiani, General 32, 78
Ségur, General Philippe-Paul de 12–13,
    45, 46, 47, 48, 60, 61, 63, 64, 69, 72,
    74, 76, 78, 82
Semenovka stream 40
Semenovskaya 57–61
Shevardino Redoubt, the 41, 43–45, 92
Siever, General Count 41, 43, 48, 57, 60
Sigismund III of Poland 19
Smolensk 29, 31, 32, 33–36, **38**, 78, 80
Smorgoni 89, **90**
Sorbier, General Jean-Barthelemot 61
Spain 5, 90
St Petersburg 27, 31, 77
Stroganov, General P. A. 49, 53
Studianka 82

tactics, French 9–10
Tarutino 76
Tilsit, Treaty of (1807) 5
Toll, Colonel Carl Friedrich von 39, 41
Tormasov, General Alexander 22, 32
Triaire, Général de Brigade Joseph **31**
Tsarevo 38
Tuchkov, General Nikolai 35, 43, 45,
    49, 53, 56
Tula 76

uniforms
    French **5**, **16**, **17**, **18**, **30**, 68
    Russian **20**, **22**, 65
Utitsa 40, 41, 45, **47**, 49, 53, 65
Uvarov, General Feodor 41, 43, **56**,
    62, 63

Valutino 35
Victor, Marshal Claude, duc de Bellune
    19
Vilna 30
Vinkovo 78
Vitebsk 31, 80
Vorontsov, General Mikhail 43, 48, 57
Vyazma 38, 79

weapons
    French **32**, 46, 47–48, 53, 61, 73, 74
    Russian **21**, 43, 44, 53, **68**, 73
Wellington, Duke of 74
Wilson, Sir Robert 13, 20, 22, 23, 36,
    37, 39, 40, 41, 43, 44, 75, 76
Wittgenstein, General Ludwig Adolf
    Peter (1769–1843) 13–14, 23, 30,
    31–32, 77, 78, 80, 82, 83
Wolzogen, Ludwig von 69
Wrede, General Carl Philipp 82
Württemberg, Eugen of 15, 33,
    57, 65